PROJECT MANAGEMENT
for
HUMAN
RESOURCES

VINCENT TUCKWOOD

66

From the smallest of local initiatives to enterprise-wide, global endeavors, HR starts every project knowing that we're dealing with the most complex element of the organization: people. Throw in the tendency to risk aversion that we share with many corporate functions, and it's easy to see how HR projects find it difficult, if not impossible, to progress.

What a breath of fresh air, then, to read this book! PROJECT MANAGEMENT FOR HUMAN RESOURCES draws upon the wisdom born from deep experience of making things work, and is presented in an easy-to-read style, with a good dose of humor, and real-world pragmatism.

Tuckwood has given us an excellent learning resource, workable toolset and in-the-trenches field guide... It should be required reading for all who aim to deliver projects in HR, and for many who already do!"

66 Congratulations! You were named as the lead resource on a very important HR initiative. The opportunity seemed so strategic that you couldn't turn it down, right? Yet here you are several months in, wondering where it all went wrong... Why are your HR colleagues not finishing assigned tasks on time? Why is your sponsor repeatedly requesting to re-schedule your project check-ins? And how is all this work going to get done without any budget (while you do your 'day job')?

In PROJECT MANAGEMENT FOR HUMAN RESOURCES, Vincent Tuckwood shares specific lessons learned in the trenches of HR, while introducing you to the basic, but fundamental, process steps and tools to set your project (and you) up for success. Regardless of your prior HR or project management experience, consider this book the required first step in your work plan!"

66 *There's a trick to making things work in HR. In fact, there are a few. Full of practical insights gleaned from real-world experience, this book nails it. If you want to get things done in Human Resources, this is how to do it."*

66 *Vince has a unique ability to bring a broad, creative and strategic perspective to situations while also being grounded in reality and help with what needs to be done in the short term. It's a wonderful balance to have in a consulting partner. I worked with Vince at Pfizer and then at my next company asked him in to help with talent strategy and analytics work. He is very adept at HR transformation work, because he's been there and led it. He approaches his work with great collaboration, compassion and flexibility."*

66

Vince is a passionate leader who has visionary ideas that inspire and motivate a team to achieve a common mission. He is a talented communicator who is personable and down-to-earth, with an immense sense of humor. I consider myself fortunate for the opportunity to be have been a part of his team.

66

I began to work with Vince in the spring of 2003 on a global HR service delivery initiative for Pfizer. Vince is honestly strategic, deeply committed and a professional who believes that teams create the best outcomes."

66

Vince is visionary. He is incredibly intelligent and capable of looking across the breadth of the HR function and determining at the macro level what long- and short-term strategic changes can be made to better meet the needs of the business.

He is extremely capable using current and emerging technologies to better align the delivery of HR services and consultation across the function.

Vince is a tremendous talent and I will not be surprised to see him recognized by external HR experts as one of the finest transformational thinkers within the HR function."

PROJECT MANAGEMENT
for
HUMAN
RESOURCES

VINCENT TUCKWOOD

PROJECT MANAGEMENT FOR HUMAN RESOURCES
The structure and art of getting things done in HR

Published by:

View Beyond LLC
20 Maple Terrace
Waterford
CT 06385
USA

ISBN: 9798641101897

FOREWORD

In early-2009, I wrote the first version of *"The Strengths Springboard - Is Your Organization Ready?"*, slap-bang in the middle of the financial meltdown that precipitated the great recession.

I remember how weird it felt to be writing a book about shifting organization cultures towards strengths-based working while talking heads the world over were predicting the end-times, and companies were shedding jobs and battening-down hatches just as fast as they could be battened!

But I wrote the book. Because what was happening in the world then could only delay the inevitability of strengths-based working. When I revisited the book for version 2 in 2017, many organizations were visibly focusing on engagement and inclusion, and taking action to make the shift. And, more recently, terms like employee experience and belonging are doing the rounds, with some CHROs being rebranded as Chief Experience Officer.

My takeaway is that, when it comes to growth, what goes around comes around. Eventually.

So, given that I already wrote and released a book just at the point the world seemed to reject its premise, it's kind of funny for me to put the final words in this book while sitting in self-isolation to protect against the spread of the COVID-19 Coronavirus - when I started writing the book, that was little more than a quiet whisper about something happening in China.

Once again, the world beyond the page is in panic, with dire predictions as to the future of work itself. And, even in the relatively short space of weeks since I began writing, I've seen HR professionals mobilizing to deal with what's happening in their client organizations, and flexing to handle issues such as remote working, temporary furloughs, etc.

Even if there's validity to the suggestion that we are entering an unprecedented new normal, it's pretty clear that the core remit of HR - alignment of people, teams and organizations to business strategy - is only going to be MORE important as we emerge.

In fact, I'd go so far as to suggest that our ability to make things happen on a wider scale and at greater pace will be tested more in the coming months and years than it ever has been before.

Compounding this is the very real possibility of an HR reduction-in-force, very similar to what happened in the immediate aftermath of the recession; HR groups shaved back to bare bones, with all non-core specialisms excised for the sake of hitting budget. It took fully 10 or so years after 2008 before I saw organizations beginning to post jobs in the the L&D and Organization Effectiveness realms - and I fully expect to see the same when the *"next normal"* settles into place

We can always learn to do ENOUGH with LESS. We know how to do that; we're good at it. That said, though my crystal ball's a bit rusty, I'm pretty confident that the *"next normal"* will be demanding that HR does FAR MORE, with FAR LESS.

You know what can help with that? Project management!

The content in this book walks the fine line between educational resource and toolkit. In providing insights from my experience, I've tried to steer clear of theoretical project management and stick to practical, pragmatic approaches that work in the field.

My aim is quite clear, to develop project management capability in the HR community, not to turn HR professionals into Project Managers.

Right now, you might be asking: *"who is this guy to tell me about project management?"*

And my answer is simply this: *I'm the guy who cares enough to challenge you to be better.*

You see, as we'll soon discuss, not only does HR lack a mindset of structured working towards specific goals, we often block or even resist progress in projects that *we have asked people to manage.*

If you're one of the lucky people who gets to work in an HR function that totally does projects awesomely, then a) what are you reading this for?; and b) please appreciate that it's not the norm.

So, who am I to tell you about project management?

I'm a battle-scarred veteran of nearly three decades of making stuff happen in HR, on both sides of the Atlantic. Along the way, I've won awards, been labeled as High Talent, and, sometimes, been stabbed in the back for delivering successful project outcomes by the very leaders who commissioned the project.

Said differently, I've successfully led projects in HR, and lived to tell the tale :)

After 20 years with Pfizer, I started my own consulting business in 2010, and in the subsequent decade, have seen that what I had experienced was far from Pfizer-specific, and an issue across my clients and wider HR network. Indeed, as soon as I mentioned writing the book with CHROs, I heard a chorus of *"YES, PLEASE!"* and *"ABOUT TIME!"*

Earlier, I mentioned strengths, and I think it's helpful here to understand that my signature Strengthsfinder® themes are: *Maximizer, Futuristic, Strategic, Communication, Activator,* and each of these also adds to the answer of why I'm writing this book.

I am here to help you grow your own capability *and* the capability of your function, by sharing hard-won lessons from delivering projects in HR. Many of these come from losses (and the subsequent learning), far more from wins. And, though this subject matter can be perceived as somewhat dry, I am a commitment to make the ride as entertaining as possible!

So, with that said, grab your planning tool of choice, and let's get going…

A PROJECT IS A TEMPORARY ENDEAVOR UNDERTAKEN TO CREATE A UNIQUE PRODUCT OR SERVICE

Project Management Institute

1: HR PROJECT MANAGEMENT HEALTH CHECK

It all comes down to a simple question:

DO YOU NEED TO IMPROVE THE PROJECT MANAGEMENT CAPABILITY OF YOUR HR FUNCTION?

Let's get the obvious out of the way, if you said *"No"*, I'm going to save you the time it takes to read this book.

If your answer is *"Yes"*, then this book is definitely for you and, though you may not need to use the simple tool I cover in this chapter, it might just help you gain further clarity on hot-spots and where you should focus attention right now.

If you don't know the answer to the question though, this chapter is really, *really* important.

Sit up, and pay attention.

Because I'm willing to bet that you do need to improve the project management capability of your HR function, even if the reasons why aren't so clear.

Let's take a look at a quick *HR Project Management Health Check*.

This takes the form of 5 simple *"Yes/No"* questions:

1. Does the project have identified scope and endpoint?
2. Is there a single, accountable Project Sponsor?
3. Is the Project Manager skilled & experienced in project management techniques?
4. Is Project Team membership limited to essential resources?
5. Are Key Stakeholders identified and assigned to an Activist*?

If one or more of these questions is a *"No"*, I'll tell you that you need to raise a RED FLAG.

If three or more of these questions are *"I don't know"*, or *"I'm not sure"*, I'll tell you that you need to raise a RED FLAG.

If more than one of these questions is an *"I don't know"*, or *"I'm not sure"*, I'll tell you to raise a YELLOW FLAG.

If ALL of the questions are a *"Yes"*, then you can raise a GREEN FLAG. Congratulations! Though you should note that this may only be a temporary celebration, because they've got to be *"Yes"* for all your projects. Period.

*NOTE: I'll describe the role of an Activist later in the book, so don't get hung up on the terminology!

So, you know the current status of project management in your HR function; you're either RED, YELLOW, or GREEN.

More importantly, you've gained valuable insight into where you may be falling short.

You see, by asking these 5 questions, we are focusing in on: *Scope, Accountability, Capability, Focus,* and *Stakeholders.*

At the highest level, these critical factors are the meat and potatoes of delivering work anywhere. It also happens that they are the indicators of what makes a successful HR project, and are consistent across our function and the disciplines it contains.

So, a quick scan of your 5 answers could give you an indicator of which factor is most at play in your project. It's even better if you can aggregate findings across multiple projects to arrive at a systemic assessment.

Is it lack of accountability?

Or maybe a failure to focus on stakeholders?

Or maybe *"All of the above"*!

When it comes to project management in HR, we'll be diving into the WHY, WHAT and HOW of all of it, so that you're able to turn things around for long-term performance.

Before we get to specifics though, we need to take a look at why project management is such a problem area for Human Resources.

1. Does the project have identified scope and endpoint?

2. Is there a single, accountable Project Sponsor?

3. Is the Project Leader skilled & experienced in project management techniques?

4. Is Project Team membership limited to essential resources?

5. Are Key Stakeholders identified and assigned to an Activist?

Answer "Yes" or "No" to each question

1 or more "No" = RED FLAG

3 or more "I don't know"/"I'm not sure" = RED FLAG

2 or more "I don't know"/"I'm not sure" = YELLOW FLAG

5 "Yes" = GREEN FLAG

hrprojmgmt.com

2: HOUSTON... WE HAVE A PROBLEM

A project is a project, right?

We know what we want to do, we plan some tasks to hit some milestones, and then we get it all done while monitoring progress. A little bit of change management and then, at some point in the future, we pat ourselves on the back for a job well done… and move on to the next thing.

A project is a project. Simple.

Yet, while that may be true for many work situations, it's not the case for HR.

I don't care what medium you choose to read - books, blogs, videos, memes - there is one consistent fact that we as a function cannot ignore: *All competitive advantage is gained through our people and how we organize them.*

We need to focus

Whichever sphere we look at - leadership, product innovation, customer engagement, strategic expansion, globalization of workforce, cultural diversity - HR, Talent & Organization Capability functions are uniquely positioned to lead, empower or, more worryingly, block the key levers of success.

Yet, while we talk a good game about all this stuff, more often than not we don't get to it because of overloaded inboxes and antiquated expectations, both internal and external to the function.

If we are to create value, we need to focus on doing that - and our focus has to be placed upon both our ongoing services AND our projects.

We have to do both to the highest levels of performance if we are to remain relevant and, ultimately, employed. Fail, and we are thrown back to the administrative Personnel function of the mid- to late-20th century.

There's a ton of stuff to do

And if that sounds like a big deal, it's because it is. I know few CHROs who want to go back to that world.

Yet, what does it take to step forward.

Well, let's start with the obvious. We are doing too much stuff.

We're involved in things that we don't need to be involved in.

We're creating unnecessary work by inefficient and ineffective processes.

We're working on antiquated systems; pen-and-paper in an app-driven landscape.

Our most valuable contributions are often relegated to the in-house equivalent of a side-gig.

And when it comes to enabling and enhancing leadership and employee experience, our reputation a) precedes us; and b) that isn't a good thing.

Through several successive eras of HR transformation, I got very used to hearing HR executives lamenting: *"we need to stop doing low value work!"* And they were right. But very few of them took steps to make that happen. Even fewer modeled that behavior in their own actions and decisions, or in the expectations they placed upon their teams.

We need to simplify processes.

We need to stop being involved in things that don't concern us.

We need to make sure our systems help Leaders, Managers and Individual Contributors do their best work.

There is no magic wand to make all this happen.

But I'll let you in on a little something…

Project management will get you close.

We need to get out of our own way

In the rest of this chapter, we're going to take a long look at the current state of project management in HR.

The issue is not that we don't know what to do, that we don't understand that there are projects that need to be delivered.

The issue is that we're not putting enough focus on using tried and tested project management tools and approaches. That we just don't employ a project management mindset across our work.

And, on the rare occasion we do, our project teams and managers often spend more time fire-fighting internal HR resistance and self-sabotage than they do advancing project objectives. Don't believe me? Ask anyone currently running an HR project. Listen carefully to what they tell you.

You see, project management is not just the things we do - the project plans, decision captures, issue logs, stakeholder management, etc. - it's how we go about doing them AND having the will to be disciplined in delivery.

We're not good at it

All of which are things that we haven't classically placed much focus upon. In fact, aside from focus upon stakeholders, we place very, very little importance upon the core building blocks of project management.

When we think of doing work, we rarely if ever focus upon the fine balance of Cost, Quality and Time. We seldom link events together in a critical path.

Few are the HR functions that place project management skills and experience on a) job descriptions; b) hiring processes, and c) career advancement decisions.

And, because we don't place a premium on project management as a function, we don't invest in its development, either at the individual or functional level.

Worse, because we kinda-sorta have an idea that our HR admins do stuff that kinda-sorta looks like project management - stuff like coordinating calendars and putting meetings together - we assume project management is an administrative task and NOT APPLICABLE to higher level HR professionals.

And, though HR admins can make awesome project managers when given the support and training to do it right, it's a really, really bad assumption that all projects should be delegated to them.

Let's look at why…

HR projects are different

Anyone who has managed projects in HR - either as a dedicated Project Manager or, more likely, as just one aspect of their overall role - knows this to be true: *HR projects are different.*

In fact, compared with many other disciplines, HR projects are not just different. Quite often, they're totally weird; if you've been managing an HR project and odd stuff has been happening, take courage - you're not alone!

HR projects often suffer from any number of the following symptoms:

- Ambiguous leadership
- Fluid budget
- Actually, NIL budget
- Unclear deliverables
- Non-specific target dates
- Silo-based work teams
- Non-involvement of target populations
- Shifting goalposts
- Risk aversion
- Change Management as an after-thought
- Non-committed project team members

- Swollen project teams to ensure involvement

- Difficulty in consensus for key decisions

- Multiple organization vetoes, used for the oddest decisions

- Failure to deliver outcomes, with little-to-no repercussions

Now, there's nothing I'd love more than to wave that mythical magic wand and make these symptoms disappear. In many ways, that's the intent of this book.

But here's the thing: *we don't get to see the world change around us without changing our own mindset and approach.*

So, before we go much further, I'm going to ask you to check your assumptions, defensiveness, and learned behaviors at the door.

Like it or not, if you've been managing projects in HR, you've been part of the system that makes those projects weird.

And if you don't like the sound of that, then there's two possibilities:

1) You've already cracked this particular nut, in which case this book may not be for you (though I really would love it if you stick around!); or…

2) You're delusional :) (I added a smiley so you'd know that I mean that with love)

Now, if you're still reading, I've got to assume that you're not delusional and you believe you can learn from this book - which is great news, since we have much to talk about.

Before we get to the meat of *WHAT* and *HOW*, I'd like to spend a little time on the more important question: *WHY?*

Why are HR projects different?

To understand why HR projects are different, we have to take a step back and consider why HR is different. And we have to reach some conclusions about our shared and accepted norms that may be uncomfortable or even difficult to swallow. In fact, I guarantee that you will come upon HR peers and leaders who will flat out refuse to agree (or admit) that these norms are in play.

Intangibles

First, let's start with the obvious. HR deals in intangibles.

While it may get dressed up by any number of descriptions - *"if it's February, it must be Human Capital Management… No, wait… That was December. This month it's Employee Experience!"* - the bottom line is that HR is concerned with some aspect of: *People, Teams & Organizations.*

Much as we would like these to be specific, tangible, repeatable, scalable, etc. they just aren't automatically so.

People are emotional - unpredictable and truly chaotic.

Teams are reactionary - forming, storming, norming and performing based upon the context within which they are placed.

Organizations are fluid - so much less formal than lines on an org chart would have us believe.

Simply put, it's really, really hard to predict what person A, in team B and organization C will do if something changes in their context as a result of something that HR does.

Don't believe it? Let's play a little thought game.

Let's say we get a recruitment campaign right, and hire a really great person for the role in hand; a sure-fire all-star. There's no way that person could ever fail, right?

And yet we see performance management cases all the time.

At best the decisions and actions taken by HR serve to reduce risk and focus the possible outcomes.

In our thought game, we can say we've significantly reduced the potential for the individual to fail in the role by selecting based upon skills, knowledge, experience and motivation. But we absolutely CANNOT say we have eliminated all risk.

Risk aversion

Which brings us to the main prevailing wind in HR: *Risk Aversion*.

Whether we recognize it or not, HR is a risk management function.

At our most transactional, we protect against the risk of bad things happening: poor performance, unwanted turnover, workplace harassment, etc.

At our most strategic we protect against the risk of unworkable strategy: workforce planning, succession, talent development, leadership readiness, etc.

As a result, it is in our fundamental nature to be risk averse and, as an observer, I would say this has only come further to the fore in HR functions since the financial crash of 2008/2009.

All of which is fine - we absolutely should seek to minimize the risks inherent in People, Team and Organization decisions. But too often, that desire tips over into a reluctance, or even fear, of upsetting the status quo.

A good example of this would be the slavish compliance to outdated, outmoded, ineffective processes such as the annual Performance Management cycle.

There isn't a person, team or organization that wouldn't breathe a sigh of relief and yell *"FINALLY!"* to hear that they were relieved of the annual trial-by-template.

Gather an HR team together and suggest getting rid of the process, though… Well, I'll let you imagine how that would go, particularly if the Performance Management process owner is in the meeting.

The behavioral norm that develops from *Risk Aversion,* at both the individual and organizational level, can be summarized as DECISION AVOIDANCE.

Said differently, unless a decision absolutely has to be made, it's much better to not make any decision, because in deciding we inherently open the door to risks of having made a bad decision.

For HR, it's better to not rock the boat than to risk Armageddon!

We are the Cobbler's children

We've already seen that we work with intangibles, and that any decision we make inevitably increases risk, so it's no surprise that HR is so often accused of not being business focused, or even standing in the way of progress.

But this isn't a *woe-is-me* tale of opinions on HR - we all live those more than enough in our day-to-day.

The proverbial Cobbler's Child has no shoes and so, for HR, we experience a norm of being so busy helping clients avoid risk, develop capability and deliver goals, that we risk our own delivery by failing to develop capability or focus upon tangible goals.

The norm for most HR professionals is an overburdened inbox and helping out whoever is shouting the loudest. And it has been that way for a LONG time. I've been in the trenches, and so have you. It's a maddening, addictive to-and-fro. Stressful, for sure.

HR has not typically hired or developed people who know how to get things done without being pushed to the limit. We have a long and proud history of rewarding the surviving hero - not the conqueror, not the visionary, but the person who keeps grinding on and doing the necessary despite the odds.

As a consequence, ANY approach to simplifying, easing, or structuring work in HR can be met with significant resistance - because it challenges the fundamental nature of both HR professionals AND the function.

In other words, we play Cobbler to our own children.

Why do HR projects fail?

We've just described the landscape in which we attempt to deliver HR projects.

We've described how our targets are intangible - an ever-evolving world of People, Teams and Organizations.

We've understood how HR is avoiding risk wherever possible.

And we've looked at how the resulting state is a function where people are doing whatever it takes just to get by, clinging on to whatever the *status quo* may be, and avoiding anything that may be perceived as rocking the boat.

Is it any wonder that the HR function has an almost comical, stereo-typical reputation amongst its business clients and the world at large?

More specifically, is it any wonder that HR projects fail more often than they succeed?

So, let's circle back to our favorite question: WHY?

The answer isn't easy to pin down - and sits at both the individual and functional levels. That said, there are three causal factors which contribute to weakness in HR Project Management: *Capability, Capacity,* and *Intent.*

In a moment, we'll dive into each of these, but here's a heads-up that after that particular discussion, we'll be paying particular attention to how the HR function self-sabotages its own projects. But first, let's look at the three causal factors.

Capability

It's too easy to say that HR doesn't hire enough Project Managers.

And I would argue that is the wrong premise anyway. It's not that we don't have enough Project Managers, it's that we don't have enough people who know how to manage projects effectively and efficiently.

I actually prefer to go further:

HR DOESN'T HAVE ENOUGH PEOPLE WHO KNOW HOW TO STRUCTURE WORK FOR OPTIMAL PERFORMANCE

What does that mean? Well, primarily it means that the majority of HR work happens in a REACTIVE stance, responding to calls, emails, calendar entries - said differently, it's dealing with *"who shouts the loudest"*.

As ever, this is not a statement of blame or judgement - it is simply an acknowledgement of the norm.

Sure, there are some who manage to step away from that stance. Chances are that they use some form of prioritization list and/or self-management rules - e.g. *"No email before lunchtime"*, etc. And if it works for them, great - they're actually the first people you should assess for readiness to manage projects.

There are 3 core capabilities that people need to be able to manage projects:

1) Anticipating, Structuring and Delivering Work

2) Conflict Adeptness/Courageous Conversations

3) People/Team Management

We're going to cover the importance of choosing the right Project Manager in the next section, but for now, let's put some simple descriptors against each of these.

Anticipating, structuring and delivering work

This is the PROACTIVE stance of looking forward…

Understanding what *will* need to be done in the future…

Estimating what it will take to get it done appropriately, and then…

Doing (or managing the doing) so that it gets done well, meeting time, cost and quality parameters.

Conflict Adeptness/Courageous Conversations

This is the major part of HOW projects are delivered in HR. A little later, we're going to talk about our function's innate desire to self-sabotage but drawing back the lens, it's clear that HR project delivery requires successful influencing of Stakeholders both within and without the function.

In other words, it's about knowing how to lead others towards, at minimum, acceptance of project outcomes and, in my experience, that is not possible without experiencing and navigating some level of conflict. For me, this is where Project Management differs from *"just getting work done"*.

As a Project Manager, there WILL come a time when you are called to go into bat for your project's progress, decisions and outcomes. You can bank on it.

People/Team Management

Unless you are part of a very, very small HR team, your project is highly likely to involve at least one other person. At minimum, that person might be a Subject Matter Expert (SME).

And, if your project team does consist of you and you alone, then I really urge you to reconsider calling it a project - by all means talk about it as *"work being done using project management methods"* but, as you'll see later in the book, that's not the same thing as running a fully-fledged project.

Once you have a project team though, it's inevitable you will have to manage individual and team performance much the same way a regular line manager does. Only you won't have as much formal authority as a hard organization reporting relationship provides.

Which is why People/Team Management is at such a premium for the successful Project Manager - when it comes to the project team, *everything* is achieved through soft-skills and influence - another reason why Conflict Adeptness/ Courageous Conversations are so important.

Capacity

Earlier, we discussed how *"surviving-despite-overwhelming-odds"* is the norm for many in HR. Given that, what do you think is the number one barrier to being involved in projects, let alone managing one?

Come on, say it with me...

"I'M TOO BUSY!"

That's right, it's our old friend *"I don't have time"* - and let me be clear, most of the time, it's not a bluff.

So, what happens is we tend to dump the project on someone who is either:

a) Visibly not busy enough (though that is rare); or...

b) Busy but coping OK (despite the fact that we only see the graceful swan above the water - never mind the ferocity of paddling beneath)

The mistake we make is not who we choose, it's that we expect them to just do the project, and we don't help them carve out the time to do that well.

In the next section, we'll look at both who we choose AND how we set them up for success.

Intent

In every organization in which I've introduced or delivered project management approaches, we've inevitably ended up at a discussion that centers on the word: *DISCIPLINE.*

Pick any situation where energy has to be applied to achieve results, and where there is an easier option that puts those very results in jeopardy - it might be dieting, exercise, behavioral changes, etc. - and you'll run into the same issue.

It takes discipline to make change stick. And, just as with any lifestyle change, it can't be down to the individual alone. It's really hard to stick to healthy eating intent when colleagues bring in cupcakes for coffee break, for example.

In fact, as soon as we step into a team or organization, the potential for better intent to be derailed increases exponentially. Any member of HR who wants to deliver successful projects will soon lose heart if their management chain, colleagues and clients don't appreciate, endorse or recognize their efforts.

Put simply, when it comes to project management in HR:

YOU HAVE TO WANT TO MANAGE PROJECTS WELL TO MANAGE PROJECTS WELL

So, the challenge with intent is to successfully encourage BOTH individuals AND the organization to want to adopt a Project Management discipline. Now, typically, this is the point where a number of self-fulfilling prophecies come into play:

- I'm too busy!

- I don't get it!

- I haven't needed to do it before, why should I start now?

- That won't work here…

- It's too restrictive…

- I would do it, but no-one wants me to…

And, if this sounds like someone avoiding a new eating regimen, or workout routine, or pattern of relationship with their partner… Well, that's the point.

We all avoid beneficial change unless we consciously commit to put the work in.

We have to INTEND to manage our projects well, and then we actually have to MANAGE our projects well.

Which takes learning - with all the discomfort and challenges that learning brings.

As with all change and learning, we have to try new things, fail a few times, tweak our approach, try again, fail again… Rinse and repeat.

And those around us have to be willing to let this happen.

This is how we grow an INTENT of project management in the HR function; how we operate with project management discipline.

In the next section of this chapter, we're going to flip our question on its head and ask how project management can succeed in HR…

But before we do, we need to rip-off the Band Aid and confront some hard truths.

We need to talk about SELF-SABOTAGE.

Self-Sabotage

I'll start by saying that this isn't a whine-fest. This isn't a pig-pile on HR. This isn't a punch on the nose for any individual in the function.

It is an honest assessment of behavioral norms that I have experienced and witnessed, and validated extensively with my network of CHROs, colleagues and clients.

Before we dive in, let's summarize:

THE PRIMARY REASON HR PROJECTS FAIL IS BECAUSE HR MAKES THEM FAIL

There. I said it. So you don't have to.

But I do ask that you take a moment to read it again and consider your own experience.

Right about now, it may be useful to actually break down what we mean by failure.

FAILURE is a loaded word. In the world of science and engineering, failure is easy to define: *something doesn't work.*

But failure in the corporate setting can be more nuanced. Failure doesn't always look like failure.

So, let's turn to the dictionary, which provides the following definitions:

- n. The condition or fact of not achieving the desired end or ends.
- n. The condition or fact of being insufficient or falling short.
- n. One that fails.

HR projects fail when they don't achieve our desired outcomes.

HR projects fail when they fall short of delivery.

But it's the last one that provides our first signal of self-sabotage.

You see, HR project failure is RARELY ascribed to an individual or leader in HR. There are always reasons: client resistance, lack of funds, compromise of project goals, lack of buy-in within the HR function... The list can (and does) go on and on.

And we have our first indicator of self-sabotage:

ABSENCE OF ACCOUNTABILITY FOR PROJECT DELIVERY IN HR

But let's circle back to the earlier definitions, because there are more subtle forces at work when it comes to project failure.

Let's look at situations where projects come up short, or fail to deliver desired ends.

In project management lingo, this can be boiled down to issues relating to SCOPE and SUCCESS CRITERIA - i.e. who/what will the project affect, and how will we know we're done.

Our primary self-sabotage here is to be *"fuzzy"* on both scope and success criteria.

When we avoid being specific about who will be affected and how, we retain a get-out clause for *"my client"*.

When we absent-mindedly shift focus mid-way through the project simply because someone somewhere raised concerns about the impact of project outcomes, we allow drift in project intent, and provide a hook for rejection of project outcomes.

When we bolt-on adjacent areas to the core project, we dilute focus and allow our now bloated project to grind to a halt. A great example of this is any process redesign project that has an interface with HRIS - e.g. Recruitment tracking,

Compensation management, Benefits administration, etc. - where, too often, changes to specific processes are folded into some *über-project* which is focused on a *"glorious future"* implementation of an all-singing-all-dancing HRIS.

Each of these provide a recipe for paralysis, and can be summarized by our second indicator of self-sabotage:

"WE CAN'T CHANGE ANYTHING UNLESS WE CHANGE EVERYTHING"

Now, let's turn our attention to the third indicator of self-sabotage - which is obvious but subtle at the same time.

Think about the period before a project is kicked off. What happens? Well, typically, there'll be a pain point - someone's finding something tough to get done, something could be improved in service offering, there's a pending change in legislation that needs to be addressed, new business strategies demand changes in core processes such as compensation, etc.

Bottom line: the call for HR projects can come from anywhere.

But HR projects are typically funneled to process owners - Recruiting ends up managing recruitment pain points, Compensation deals with pay issues, etc, etc, etc.

And that generally works... UNTIL we form the project team. Because suddenly every HR leader in the place wants *"their person"* involved. Suddenly we're talking co-leads and extended project teams. Suddenly, every project decision has to be validated and endorsed by every HR team in the organization.

Suddenly the *"person in the room"* is spending time and focus obstructing project progress on behalf of the *"people outside the room"*.

And they're getting patted on the back for doing so.

This is our third - and most important - signal of self-sabotage:

WE INVOLVE PEOPLE IN PROJECTS IN ORDER TO PROTECT AGAINST PROJECT DELIVERABLES

We're drawing to the end of our section on *Why Do HR Projects Fail?*

We've covered quite a lot of ground, identifying 3 core causal factors that affect us at both the individual and functional levels:

1) We don't have the CAPABILITY

2) We don't have the CAPACITY

3) We don't have the DISCIPLINE of INTENT

These show up in different ways, but are typically at the core of all project failure.

In addition, we've looked at the thorny issue of self-sabotage - the main behavioral factor undermining projects in HR.

We've identified 3 clear signals of self-sabotage:

1) Absence of accountability for project delivery in HR

2) "We can't change anything unless we change everything"

3) We involve people in projects in order to protect against project deliverables

All of which are in play more often than they are not.

When it comes to HR project management, most of the time, we really are our own worst-enemy.

But it's time to move away from the negative. We are rapidly approaching a pivot point in this book. And while we may dip back into these constructively critical waters to make a point, we're largely done with lamenting the current state of HR projects.

Thankfully, there are remedies for self-sabotage. The approach, framework and tools presented in the rest of this book will go a long way towards neutralizing damaging behaviors as, or even before, they happen.

So, without much ado, let's ask a much more interesting question: *WHAT MAKES HR PROJECTS SUCCEED?*

What makes HR projects succeed?

Well, we've covered a lot of ground that could provide fuel for pessimism. Thankfully, there's no need to despair: *HR PROJECTS CAN SUCCEED!*

In the remainder of this introductory chapter, we'll look at the key factors that underpin success of project management in the HR function.

But before we do, let's get the biggest one out of the way because, while it shouldn't need to be said... It needs to be said!

The most important factor in successful HR project management is…

TREAT HR PROJECTS AS IF THEY ARE PROJECTS!

Nothing else matters until that is accepted, endorsed and lived in the real world. It is the first step in adopting a project management mindset; the first commitment to our new-found discipline.

So, once that's in place, what else do we need to make things work?

Understanding the landscape

Business landscape

Earlier we looked at how the HR function focuses upon the key levers of competitive advantage.

So, it follows that successful HR projects deliver new products or services that fit the business landscape - both in terms of outcomes and change impact.

Successful HR projects frame their deliverables, activities and decisions within the business landscape. These are not HR projects *"done unto"* the business, they are business projects delivered by HR.

People, Organization & Culture landscape

So, HR projects start out with a business framing of expectations. But the road is littered with projects that were formed on the whim of executives chasing the latest flavor-of-the-month best practice, or career-advancing pet goal. In fact, I would go so far as to say that, arguably, HR has been following best-practice publications drawing upon Jack Welch's tenure as CEO of GE for over 25 years.

As with any successful consulting interaction, the most important thing is to understand scope, and define expectations before we begin. We must bring professional rigor to these early discussions, and avoid blindly chasing the presenting symptom.

As a consequence, when we are asked to implement a people practice, we must have an OPINION on what's been done elsewhere, both within our company and in the wider world of practice - what's worked and, importantly, what hasn't.

If we don't know enough to have an opinion, we must be prepared to put in the research work to form one.

After all, just because it COULD be done, doesn't mean it SHOULD be done.

HR landscape

And yet, we must be careful as we research what has happened elsewhere, because one of the major self-sabotage refrains can show up: *"That won't work here..."*

This is the voice of the *status quo*, the defense of the risk-averse, the culture writ large.

So, while we can appreciate that not every project is well-founded, and may have an opinion that the project should not happen, we cannot afford to knee-jerk our response.

As we have seen in the previous section, this knee-jerk response is largely due to a risk aversion response in the HR function.

And successful HR projects take this into account by understanding, and addressing their own internal stakeholder management as well as that beyond the function.

For example, let's say we're planning a project to change governance of the compensation cycle:

Should it be led by the compensation function? If so, to what extent do we need to involve HR Business Partners? Representing which areas of the business? And how much should HRIS specialists be involved? How might any changes affect those HR colleagues currently engaged in processing payroll changes?

In the space of a short paragraph of questions, I've given food for at least a few hours worth of meetings and discussion. Yet, I haven't even touched on the wider output of the project and how it will affect employees, managers and senior leaders.

Every question I asked concerns the HR landscape. And successful HR projects anticipate such questions, prepare to address the answers, and monitor developments throughout their life-cycle.

Commitment to strong governance

We have seen how successful HR projects pay close attention to the landscape in which the project will deliver.

They are business projects delivered by HR.

They take account of what has and hasn't been tried in the internal and external world of practice.

And they anticipate the impact upon, and potential resistance from internal HR stakeholders.

While these three factors are essential to success, they only come alive when there is a commitment to strong project governance.

Simply put, governance is how decisions get made in the project.

We're going to dive into governance in a big way in the next chapter, so for now I'll summarize:

STRONG PROJECT GOVERNANCE MEANS MAKING DECISIONS AT THE NECESSARY LEVEL, WITH APPROPRIATE INVOLVEMENT OF IMPACTED STAKEHOLDERS

When we observe successful HR projects, we see a pattern of *"decision-made, move-on"* - and a track record of seldom needing to revisit decisions, because they were well made in the first place.

Remember how HR involves people in projects in order to protect against project deliverables? Avoiding and complicating decisions are where that symptom most comes to life.

Successful HR projects prepare for that, influence through it, and use tools to reinforce the point.

Choosing the right Project Manager

Given the landscapes in which we operate, and the governance we choose, the single-most important factor in successful HR projects is who we choose to manage the project.

Yes, that's right - despite all the prevailing winds, it all comes down to an individual.

Or maybe that should be *because* of the prevailing winds, it all comes down to an individual.

And I'll let you in on a little secret: the primary screening criteria is NOT a project management certification.

THE PRIMARY SCREENING CRITERIA FOR HR PROJECT MANAGERS IS CREDIBILITY

Why credibility?

Well, we said it earlier: HR projects are different. In fact, we didn't just say it, we covered it in very great depth!

Given everything we discussed there, which ultimately can be summarized in the term *"self-sabotage"*, it should hopefully be clear that an HR Project Manager is going to spend a large proportion of their time managing both HR team members AND HR stakeholders. In fact, this will be the case more than managing stakeholders external to HR.

If your HR Project Manager doesn't have credibility within your HR function, they are already starting way behind the curve.

And it's a huge risk to assume that a non-credible Project Manager will be able to earn credibility through delivering the project. Possible? Yes. Probable? Only maybe. And even less so if it's a particularly thorny project.

In the next chapter, we're going to spend a good chunk of time on how to reach a decision on who should manage a project.

For now, though, let's summarize by simply saying this:

GIVEN THE CHOICE, IT IS MUCH
BETTER TO TEACH A CREDIBLE HR
PROFESSIONAL HOW TO MANAGE
PROJECTS, THAN TO TEACH A
CREDIBLE PROJECT MANAGER ABOUT
HUMAN RESOURCE MANAGEMENT

Well, we've spent quite a bit of time looking at the presenting issue of project management in HR.

We know that we need to focus, because there's a ton of stuff to do, and we need to get out of our own way. We also know that we're not very good at it.

We've seen how HR projects are different, largely because we deal in intangibles, spend a lot of time avoiding risk, and we're usually the last to heed our own best advice.

In looking at why HR projects fail, we discussed issues of capability, capacity and discipline of intent. Put together these result in a very unhealthy norm of self-sabotage in HR projects.

Luckily, though, we've been able to identify core factors that make HR projects succeed.

By understanding the complex landscape in which the project will operate, and committing to strong governance, we've seen that business projects delivered by HR are much more likely to succeed.

And that, when such projects are managed by HR professionals with the credibility to influence HR peers and leaders, the chances of success increase drastically.

So, Houston... Do we have a problem?

Yes. We do.

But thankfully, there are clear, workable, scalable solutions.

The rest of this book is ALL about that!

3: PROJECT MANAGEMENT BASICS

What is a project?

"A temporary endeavor undertaken to create a unique product of service."
(Project Management Institute)

"A unique set of co-ordinated activities with definite starting and finishing points, undertaken by an individual or organization to meet specific objectives within defined schedule, cost and performance parameters."
(BS-6079 - Guide to Project Management)

What is Project Management?

The application of knowledge, tools and techniques…

… to the direction and co-ordination of human and material resources…

… throughout the life-cycle of a project…

… in order to achieve stakeholder satisfaction at delivery.

Project focus

As we can see, a project is always balancing Time, Cost and Quality (Performance) parameters.*

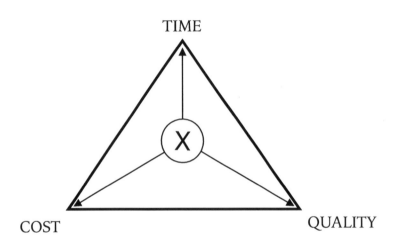

In general, any HR project will have all three parameters in play - typically, however, one will predominate.

NOTE: in many projects, particularly in industrial manufacturing or public works, a fourth parameter is added - SAFETY. However, this is less prevalent in HR, and we can assume that any safety parameters can be included in QUALITY

Single-parameter Projects

Time-bound Project

Primarily concerned with delivering to a specific deadline or timeline, this project may be willing to spend on resources and/or compromise quality/performance standards.

Cost-bound Project

Primarily concerned with delivering to a budget, this project may be willing to delay deliverables and/or compromise quality/performance standards."

Quality-bound Project

Primarily concerned with delivering to a specific level of quality/performance, this project may be willing to spend on resources and take longer to achieve deliverables.

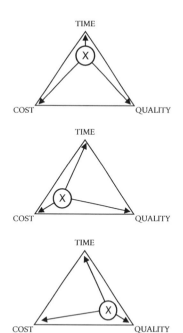

Multi-parameter Projects

Cost- & Time-bound Project

This project could be categorized as "quick, cheap and dirty", compromising quality/performance in order to hit deadlines and budget.

Time- & Quality-bound Project

This project could best be described as "do it right, no matter the cost", where budget stretches to make sure deadlines are hit, and highest quality/performance is achieved.

Cost- & Quality-bound Project

This project could best be described as "do it right, eventually", where budget is constrained but quality/performance standards are non-negotiable.

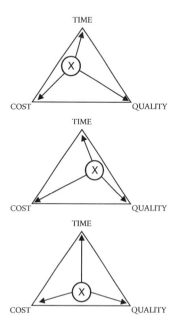

Is it a Project, or is it a Program?

As projects grow bigger and encapsulate more, and more diverse, work-streams, there comes a point where it makes sense to sub-divide the project into several projects, possibly with multiple project managers, under a single umbrella.

In this situation, the collection of projects is no longer termed a project, it has morphed into a Program. Program Management is a separate topic to that covered in this book, and subject to its own methods and approaches. At minimum, a Project will be expected to report status to a Program Management Office (PMO) or similar role/organization.

Project management approaches

There are many approaches to organizing and delivering projects - almost as many as there are Project Managers - starting from the traditional waterfall that is the focus of this book, through to more recent developments such as AGILE, PRINCE, Lean, 6-Sigma, etc.

These newer approaches were developed to meet specific challenges, typically from manufacturing and/or software development, and often blur the line between project management and process re-engineering - with a focus upon specific, granular data that is often impossible to gather for HR initiatives.

As it stands, the traditional approach to project management is sufficient for over 95% of likely HR projects, and using a higher level technique will prove to be overkill.

As with any specialism, there is depth and nuance to the subject, much of which is outside our scope - remember, our aim is to teach HR professionals to better manage projects, not turn them into masterful Project Managers.

In the event you do come across a project that fits a more advanced model and is rich with specific data, you would be well advised to engage a certified professional in that approach rather than trying to do it *"in-house"*.

WHAT STARTS
WELL ENDS
BETTER

4: BEFORE YOU DO ANYTHING

Have you ever heard of the saying *"Ready... Aim... Fire..."*?

Well, sad to say, but the majority of HR projects are better classified as *"Fire... Ready... Aim..."*

Said differently, the combination of being very busy, wanting to add value, and wanting to reduce risk, can very quickly move us to action without putting in the necessary thought or consideration of whether what we want to do makes sense, or even has a hope of solving the presenting problem.

It really is a knee-jerk reflexive action: *"See a problem? Start fixing it!"*

Have you ever been working on a project only to find that someone else is working on something very similar - maybe in a part of HR serving another part of the business, or in a different region or country?

The first time I was asked to form a Program Management Office, guess how many projects were already underway across our 5 site, 125 person HR organization?

149 PROJECTS

Let that sink in for a moment: *there were more projects than members of HR.*

And that didn't count projects coming from partnership with other divisions, or from the corporate headquarters.

That was just what had been generated by our own function, and it was the reason I was asked to form the Program Management Office. Just to be clear, I don't highlight this group because this was an abnormal state of affairs - I've found this ratio typical of HR functions of all sizes and industries

Within 1 month, through structured triage, including use of the Health Check presented earlier in the book, we were down to 47 projects - having merged, collapsed or just plain closed over 100 projects.

And, from subsequent experience, these ratios hold pretty true - nearly everyone has their own pet project, and about two-thirds of them aren't justified at all.

Defining an HR project

Given this, there's a really obvious, simple question that we need to ask, that rarely seems front-of-mind...

Is it even a project?

I introduced this book with a very, very important definition. You might have skipped over it, so let's repeat it, because it's literally THAT important!

A PROJECT IS A TEMPORARY ENDEAVOR UNDERTAKEN TO CREATE A UNIQUE PRODUCT OR SERVICE

This comes from the Project Management Institute (PMI); the people who literally wrote the book (Project Management Book of Knowledge, or PMBOK for short) on the subject.

I can't stress how important it is that you know and understand this definition. For a Project Manager, this is earth, air, fire and water; it's bedrock.

To be blunt, if your project ain't this, it ain't a project!

So, please go back and read it multiple times; highlight it; copy it into your personal notebook; set a reminder on your phone to flag it for your attention every Monday morning.

Why? Because of those 100 projects that we removed in the first month, over sixty percent failed this definition. What was being called a project was, more often than not, nowhere near actually being a project.

To explain how this triage works, let's break the definition down, because it has several moving pieces.

"A project is…"

In the spirit of keeping things really, really simple we'll hold to what the meaning of the word *"is…"* is.

It's not *"A project might be…"*

Or *"A project could…"*

It's *"A project is…"*

And, if you're going to improve the quality of project management in your HR function, you have to decide, truly DECIDE, that you are going to manage projects, not things that are not projects.

This is the first step of adopting a project management discipline, and it precedes everything that follows.

"… a temporary endeavor…"

And here we come to a major stumbling block for many HR projects.

If the piece of work that's being called a project doesn't have a clearly defined, communicated and accepted start- and end-point, guess what?

That's right, it ain't a project!

Projects are NOT day-to-day work. Nor are they ongoing service delivery.

A project only exists for its own lifetime and, inherent in that premise, a project will ALWAYS go away.

As an aside, I'm always cautious about anyone who claims a project be included by name in their job description by way of recognizing contribution - because this assumes the project continues for the lifetime of that job. Better to say *"manages appropriate projects…"* to indicate the skill-set and experience needed, but try to avoid enshrining any project as *"everlasting"*.

"… undertaken to create a unique product or service"

Well now, that's quite specific, isn't it?

Where once there was the absence of *something*, one day there will be *something*. The project is the means by which that *something* becomes a reality.

It really is that cut-and-dried.

There was a need…

… And a project delivered a solution…

… And so the need was met…

… And so, the project ended.

Simple.

Before I get too militant though, I need to confess that, in this instance, I'm willing to flex.

Remember in the last chapter when we discussed how and why HR projects are different? Well, the net impact of that experience demands that I personally allow a little fuzziness to creep in.

You see, not everything is a matter of *"creating"*, for HR sometimes it's a matter of *"delivering"* - now, as I mentioned, I'm not talking about ongoing work here, but there *is* a significant subset of HR service delivery that can benefit massively from project management discipline.

Some examples include:

- Talent Planning Process
- Succession Reviews
- Compensation Calibration
- Recruitment Campaigns

What makes these examples similar? Well, it all goes back to the first part of the definition: *a temporary endeavor…* You see, they each have a start- and end-point and, once complete, they won't exist again - at least not immediately, if they're on an annual or semi-annual cycle

But let me ask you a question: What proportion of these, or similar finite work, does your function currently deliver using project management techniques?

I'd be willing to hazard a guess that most of the time, the closest it gets to project management is a calendar of key deadlines. And, in many instances, the delivery is a black-box - assigned to one person who just gets on and does it.

When I led recruitment, we developed an approach where each recruitment campaign was delivered as a project, with tasks and milestones, resource forecasting, pre-arrangement of interview dates, etc. Within a year, recruitment had gone from a just-in-time, fly-by-the-seat-of-your-pants thrill-ride, to a well-oiled machine. Along with changes in how we behaved in every interaction stage of the process, we successfully doubled application rate, quadrupled offer rate, and got to 98% acceptance rate from first-choice candidates. In the same period we reduced advertising spend by around 15%.

Bottom line, delivering specific finite work using project management techniques can significantly improve the overall performance of your HR function.

But of course it's a project!

Look, I understand... but, is it really? Really?!

It may feel a little theoretical to use the PMI definition to assess whether a piece of work counts as a project - especially given the fact that I've already pointed out there is some fuzziness inherent in typical HR work.

So, let me be clear, the triage we just discussed is most useful in assessing things that are already ongoing - just like my experience of trimming down 149 projects by 60%.

Now, you're not going to do that every day - I certainly haven't - so it's better for us to look at how and why projects spin-up.

Someone just getting their work done

We've already covered how day-to-day work and process delivery in HR can be delivered as projects if we decide to take that approach. But there is a looser version of this, which is simply due to someone getting their work done, who decides it would be really good to involve some people.

Have you ever been invited to a meeting where one person seems to be doing all the talking, and not really seeking your input, involvement, decision, or action? It can feel like that person is seeking permission for their own decisions, justification for taking action, or simply playing CYA!

All of which is understandable, if a little annoying.

The problem comes in the moment when that person uses the term *"team"*…

Let me give you an example. When I was heading up recruitment, the New Colleague Orientation program was owned and delivered by our Learning & Development function. Members of my team (and I) would present one of the sessions - to close out the hiring process, and welcome the colleagues that we had successfully recruited. It was our official stamp of *"we're done!"*

Only a strange thing began to happen - when the facilities group rep wanted to add content to the first week program, they came and asked me, because I happened to have hired the second-in-command in Facilities Management, who had pointed the rep in my direction.

I, naturally, did a warm handover to the colleague in Learning & Development who owned the program.

This happened a couple of times with different content owners.

And suddenly, the meeting appeared on my calendar - in amongst back-to-back interviews.

I make it to the meeting. And have a rich discussion about New Colleague Orientation. No action is delegated to me. I don't have to make any decision. I'm asked for, and provide, feedback on changes being suggested to content.

The meeting ends, and I get back to interviewing.

Only… Another meeting pops up. Actually, it was a series of weekly meetings. Given the amount of interviews running at the time, I asked what was going on. And, sure enough, I was now a member of the New Colleague Orientation Project Team.

I hadn't been asked if I wanted to do it. I hadn't been asked if I thought it needed a project, or even a team.

Bottom line, I was a concerned stakeholder, and wanted nothing but success for colleagues going through the program. Yet here I was, a member of a team that was in place simply to support someone actually doing their job.

As an aside, over time, it became clear that my involvement here was being driven not just by personal choice, but by deeper organization political currents between HR and Learning & Development - remember when I said how HR involves people in projects to protect against projects? Yeah, that comes from experience!

I use this as a simple example of how projects can spin-up without very much effort or intent. And once a thing becomes a thing, it has a nasty habit of continuing to be a thing!

Pain points

This is, I think, the primary reason that projects start in HR. We hear about, or experience, a pain point, and immediately start running to fix things.

It's completely understandable - most people are in the HR function because they want to add value, and they want to help people and the business. And, as we've discussed, HR colleagues are already very, very busy.

However, these factors can come together with explosive results when it comes to projects.

Let me use an example that I think many of us have experienced, witnessed or heard tell of.

In 1993, we ran our first employee attitude survey. Back in those days, the survey was over 90 questions covering classical Hertzberg Hygiene and Motivator Factors.

I won't go into long detail on the survey here, but I will draw attention to one question that scored remarkably low across all demographics and organization sub-sections: *"Poor performance is effectively managed in my work-group"*.

A significant chunk of the organization did not agree with this statement - in fact, only around a third of respondents were positive. Put simply, it was the very definition of a *pain-point*.

Fast forward several YEARS later.

The Global Performance Management project formed in response to that question, and drawing upon best practices elsewhere in industry, is still debating matters such as whether the rating scale should be 3-point, 5-point, or 7-point. There are vigorous debates as to whether a manager should share rating information with a colleague before change in compensation is agreed. A strategic decision whether to customize PeopleSoft's core performance management module is being tee-d up over a series of meetings.

Now, I'm not here to debate whether that project was the right or wrong thing to do, nor how effectively the project was managed. I use the example to show how a clear pain-point can be the jumping off point for a multi-year, sprawling project that may, or may not, ever address the pain.

In this case, the issue was not one of templates and practice - for around half of our managers the resulting process and system was a retrograde impact upon their approach to managing - it slowed them down and confused things. And those managers who didn't manage well managed only slightly better, if at all, under the new process and system.

And survey upon survey told us that opinion was NOT shifting.

In fact, even a little scholarship would have shed light upon the stubborn fact that this question (or variant thereof) rarely, if ever, receives positive feedback. The issue is one of accountability - and it is at the heart of management. And no amount of templates, process steps, guidelines, training, system capture, etc. can hold someone accountable.

Instead of knee-jerking to a *"fix everything"* project solution, we might have had greater impact on performance by choosing instead to act as a strong mirror to leaders and managers, using data to support their improved management.

But that doesn't sound like a project, doesn't give the immediate dopamine hit of swift action to respond the pain-point, and it doesn't let HR proudly point out how it is responding to the survey feedback.

Put bluntly:

STARTING A PROJECT FEELS LIKE A WIN, EVEN IF THAT PROJECT IS DOOMED TO FAIL

But wait… I have an idea!

So, we've looked at how projects can spin-up just from people doing their work and involving people unnecessarily, and as a quick reaction to presenting pain-points.

These two categories capture around 80% of HR-projects-that-never-should-have-been. The remainder are described in our final category: *someone somewhere has an idea.*

It doesn't matter whether it's a business leader, the CEO, CHRO, visiting consultant, but someone, somewhere thinks they have an insight into something that will make business run better.

It might be an inflight magazine, a conference, a chance meeting on a train, but that latest, greatest *"best practice"* is out there somewhere.

Or maybe, it's the HR rep who has recently attended training on an assessment approach and who now sees that assessment as potentially fundamental to literally *every* process in HR, so kicks off all the projects necessary to rewrite everything!

We've all seen it happen. And, we've all been guilty of it. It's human nature to take our opinion on the state of affairs and believe we have the answer.

But only in HR do we allow that - ripe as it is with confirmation bias, recency bias and law-of-small-numbers - to become a project without applying any critical filters.

These pet projects can rapidly swell - particularly if they are associated with organizational or individual status. It is, after all, the brave CHRO that tells the CEO that their idea doesn't have merit. Much easier to say *"we'll give it a try"* and then let it wither on the vine.

After all, we can always blame the project team, or even just business climate, just so long as we don't have to say *"No"*.

Knowing the difference

So, we've looked at where HR projects come from:

- Delivering work

- Addressing pain points

- Someone's idea

And, despite my warnings, that ain't about to change.

The question is not one of *"How do we stop HR projects forming based on these things?"*, but instead, *"How do we decide if an HR project should form based upon the presenting issue?"*

And that, right there, is the secret key to the gates of great HR project management, because: *What Starts Well Ends Better!*

We've covered a lot of ground to say that we must know the difference between what requires an HR project and what doesn't.

So, without further ado, let's boil it down to the most important question you need to ask before you do *anything*:

WHAT ARE WE PLANNING TO DO, AND WHY DO WE WANT TO DO IT?

To quote the board game Monopoly, if you don't have the answers, then DO NOT PASS GO!

Project governance

So far in this chapter, we've covered the WHY of HR projects. And everything after this chapter is going to be a deep-dive into the WHAT and HOW of project management.

That leaves us with one critical area that must be addressed before you do anything.

The WHO of project management.

Who sanctions it?

Who guides it?

Who does it?

Who else is involved?

In short, we can term this *Project Governance*.

Now, the G-word is typically reserved for formal decision-making structures, but I'd like you to keep it firmly in mind to cover all aspects of activity and decision-making.

And, though it may feel a little counter-intuitive, the first, most important step in project governance is not to identify the Project Manager.

The first, most important step is to identify and task the *Project Sponsor*.

Sponsorship

I'll say it clearly, sponsorship is the single-most important factor in ensuring a successful project in HR. In fact, for HR, it's *imperative*.

A Project Sponsor contributes executive direction to the project team, providing an *"umbrella"* within which the team can operate to achieve agreed deliverables throughout the project life-cycle.

Sponsors may be called upon to resolve escalated issues, provide vision, guidance and reassurance to project team members, and even make executive decisions relating to risks affecting, or arising from, the project.

Put bluntly, when it comes to the project, the buck stops with the Sponsor.

Once we dive into the specifics of how to manage projects, you'll hear a lot more about what a Sponsor does, and how it happens.

Right now, though, we're going to look at some of the common sticking points when it comes to sponsorship, because things can go very wrong if you don't make strong decisions when it comes to who you choose as your sponsor.

Individual vs. joint

Earlier, we talked about self-sabotage of HR projects. One of the quickest, and clearest, places this can happen is the moment that a project is assigned multiple sponsors.

Now, as with most self-sabotage, this often isn't a conscious act. What happens in HR is the executive version of the *"involvement game"* we've already covered. The thinking goes like this: *"if the project is sponsored by both these people, then they'll both be committed to making it work!"*

And, sometimes, that plays out beautifully. Sometimes. More often though, the project is snared within competing internal politics, wrangling, and the ever-so-sticky *status quo*.

You can probably tell, I'm no fan of joint sponsorship.

What I've seen at play is an overwhelming assumption that all executive leaders play nice together.

Even the slightest self-honesty tells us that is false. It just is.

So basing sponsorship decisions upon this assumption is pretty much a sure-fire route to damaging the performance of your project.

In my experience though, it gets much worse than that, with projects grinding to a standstill, having to revisit long-closed deliverables, and/or produce multiple versions of communication materials.

If you need an analogy, being a Project Manager with joint sponsors often feels like being a kid wanting to do the right thing, but caught between two acrimonious parents.

At its root, choosing to deploy joint sponsorship is an accountability-dodge, and definitely part of the symptom set we covered earlier, so please, if you're tempted to go this route, challenge yourself, and challenge yourself *hard,* before you do.

Individual vs. Steering Committee/Leadership Team

So, you know that I'm no fan of joint sponsorship. So go on, I dare you, ask me what I think about asking the whole HR Leadership Team to sponsor a project…

Yeah… er, NO.

This is Joint Sponsorship on steroids!

By all means, assign the HR Leadership Team to be a key stakeholder group, or key individual stakeholders - we'll be talking about that a LOT when we get to stakeholder management.

If your CHRO is adamant that they want the HRLT positioned this way, then a quiet, behind-closed-doors conversation needs to happen because, in this situation, the CHRO is your Sponsor. Period. And they need to know that.

Similarly, a wider Steering Committee can be a very useful group of stakeholders. But they should not be considered to hold a sponsorship role. They may guide, they may enable, they may advocate, but they aren't you Sponsor.

Business vs. HR

Having made my case that sponsorship should be individual in order to enforce accountability, I want to add one final note on a situation where joint sponsorship *may* be justified; an exception to the rule.

I have seen *some* HR projects work with both an HR sponsor AND a business sponsor. One that immediately comes to mind is organization cultural change, which should rarely, if ever, be led completely from the HR function.

In this case going for joint sponsorship is as much about symbology as it is about tactics. It's just very, very important to have business leaders who are saying *"Yes, I am choosing to make this happen…"*

But, at a deeper level, it can be useful to have a business leader sponsoring key projects because, as we've already discussed, HR tends to pull back from risk and avoid change, and this happens to HR leaders too. Having a business leader to keep your HR Sponsor on track can be very useful when the rubber hits the road; or when something else hits the fan.

Be careful, though, because there can be a tendency to ask a business leader to co-sponsor every aspect of HR work. Sooner or later that makes no sense, and HR has to have courage in its own work and leadership.

Or, in other words, HR has to be held accountable for its projects.

ROLE OF A PROJECT SPONSOR

A Project Sponsor contributes executive direction to the ProjectTeam, providing an *"umbrella"* within which the team can operate to achieve agreed project deliverables. Specifically:

Before Project

- Establishes a clear future state vision to enable the Project Manager and Project Team to plan, prioritize, and assess completion
- Provides coaching and feedback to develop capability of Project Team members
- Advocates for the purpose and aims of the project

Initiation

- Empowers the Project Team, maintaining minimal, appropriate involvement in detail/tasks
- Represents the Project Team and aims in discussions with Key Stakeholders
- Provides go/no-go decision to proceed with the proposed Project Charter

Planning

- Makes decisions regarding acceptable risk thresholds
- Demonstrates active sponsorship by conducting courageous discussions with stakeholders and the Project Manager to achieve the objectives of the project
- Provides go/no-go approval of project & stakeholder management plans

Implementation

- Responds to escalated issues regarding scope, time, cost and quality in a timely and decisive manner
- Reinforces Project Team accountability through constructive feedback
- Provides go/no-go approval of final project deliverables

Completion

- Provides visible recognition and penalties to reinforce the project objectives and desired change
- Provides performance and development feedback to Project Manager

Who should manage the project?

There, now that's an easy question to answer: *someone who knows how to manage projects.*

Right. Let's move on to the next chapter…

All kidding aside, it should go without saying that, unless you're really into deep-immersion development experiences, your Project Manager will have at least some capability to manage projects.

Remember, we've already put one major caveat on the table - your Project Manager must have sufficient credibility in both HR work AND the HR function.

Even with that fully understood and accepted, there are a couple of additional sticking points that I've witnessed in HR.

Beware the resumé

Sadly, our function - like many others - suffers from resumé padding. And one of the clear areas where this is most prevalent comes from our earlier discussion on self-sabotage.

You see, as we've already noted, *HR involves people in projects to protect against project deliverables.* As a result, we often have many people involved in projects.

And, as we all know, not all involvement should be considered equal.

So, when reviewing potential candidates, internal or external, be careful of claims to experience of leading, managing or being part of projects. And, in selecting the right person, make sure to assess whether the candidate did, in fact, manage the project!

It may feel like the easiest way to spot a credible Project Manager is to ask the person currently doing the work in question to manage the project.

For example, let's take a project to make changes in relocation policy, process and practice. Easy, you may think, we'll ask our Relocation Specialist to manage the project; after all, no-one knows the relocation policy nearly as well as them!

Hold your horses.

Subject matter expertise does NOT necessarily equal project management expertise. It can happen, in which case you should definitely go for it, but it's far from a safe assumption.

The primary role of a Project Manager is to structure work into a plan, and then ensure everything goes to plan, and handle things when it doesn't. While also ensuring stakeholders are appropriately involved and briefed. And managing the Project Team, there's that too.

None of which, in our example, bears any resemblance to relocation policy, process or practice.

In fact, if our Relocation Specialist is truly the point person for all things relocation, then there's a good chance they'll be a hindrance as Project Manager, because of the tendency to need them down in the weeds of detail. It's really tough to stay outside and inside the work of a project all at once.

Which doesn't even cover what happens if the Relocation Specialist disagrees with project deliverables like automation, etc. Nothing like a change-resistant Project Manager to grind things into the dust.

Once again, we're back at our early discussion around self-sabotage. If you absolutely must ask the Relocation Specialist to manage the relocation project,

SELECTING THE RIGHT PROJECT MANAGER

Can they do the job?

- Experience in managing projects of appropriate scale and complexity to the project you're considering?
- Successful track record of project delivery to Cost, Quality & Time criteria
- Experience of assessing stakeholder needs, current state and building appropriate change management and communication plans
- People and team management (preferred)
- Project management certification from a recognized provider (preferred)

Will they do the job?

- Ability to prioritize project management alongside current "day-job"
- Uses project management techniques to deliver day-to-day work
- Project management experience is identified specifically as a development aim

Will they fit in?

- Credibility within the HR function and wider stakeholders, or the potential to rapidly build such credibility
- Ready to make tough calls to advance project despite potential resistance from colleagues
- Knowledge of project subject matter
- Ability to influence people at all levels of the organization, and beyond immediate sphere of control

hrprojmgmt.com

stop for a moment and consider whether you're actually just asking them to do their job differently. In which case, is it really a project?

So, with all those caveats and observations in place, take a look at *"Selecting The Right Project Manager"*.

Clearing The Runway

Well, we're nearing the end of this chapter about what needs to happen before anything happens!

We've talked about defining the project, the role of the Sponsor and wider governance, and how to actually select the Project Manager who's going to get things done.

But before we actually get moving on the project itself, there are some final factors that need to be in place if you want to give yourself the best chance of success.

Let me speak to the Project Sponsor right now, okay?

Remember, the prevailing wind in HR is to try to slow, deny, or avoid project outcomes so, make no mistake, in asking a member of HR to manage a wider project in HR, you are setting down a potential landmine of organization politics, particularly if you are deploying a fairly junior member of HR as a developmental assignment.

And, though you may be a Big Kahuna in your function, with serious political clout, it's not simply enough to select the Project Manager and say: *"get going"*.

You see, Project Managers don't fail spectacularly, they fail by corrosion over time:

- Their current manager downplays the time and resource they need to deliver the project
- SMEs withhold or delay information and/or resources that the project requests
- HR leaders refuse to commit to project activities and/or decisions
- Project Team members choose (or are forced to choose) to de-prioritize project work

I have seen all of these in their malignant glory, and it's not a pretty sight.

As a Project Sponsor, your role is to ensure the appointment of this Project Manager is respected and supported by their current Manager, HR leaders, SMEs and Project Team members.

And it must happen before a single project activity takes place.

In the main, this means that you have to clear the runway, making sure the Project Manager is given time and space to deliver the project. This may even mean considering partial, or even full, backfills for their "day-job"

It's really important at this stage, that you are not a sponsor-in-name-only - please do not leave the discussion between the Project Manager and their own manager. It has to be a 3-way discussion, with you making clear that there are formal expectations of time and resource commitment from the Project Manager.

As an added spin, you must also set an expectation that the current Manager will NOT have jurisdiction over the project or deliverables due to reporting relationship.

Why am I so firm on this? Because, sadly, there will always come a point where you need to circle back with the current Manager when they pull the Project Manager away from the project. And, make no mistake, you may have to be VERY assertive in these discussions.

Ensuring Project Manager time and focus is critical, and nearly as important is the same conversation with regard to Project Team members and their own managers.

Basically, you are carving out the space for the project to operate, and the expectation that that space is respected and protected.

As an aside, for highly sensitive projects, these discussions may also include a ring-fence in terms of confidentiality and access, specifically blocking the current Manager from insight into project content.

It is totally within your role to position the imminent project with fellow HR leaders, and you should not leave this action to the Project Manager after things kick off.

Unfortunately, several times, I've been in the situation where I've walked into a meeting with an HR leader, ready to talk stakeholder engagement in their client group, only to be met with *"wait, what is this all about?"* leaving me wondering how the project could have secured funding and approval before I was even asked to manage it!

And, finally, there's the HR function, always a fine balance of awareness vs. full briefing. For me, SMEs in the project content area need to know the project is happening and how they may be involved, or asked for input. The wider function really needs awareness only - i.e. *"this is happening…"* Too much information, and everyone wants to have input and/or be directly involved, bringing us back to the core pathology of our self-sabotage.

Now, with all that preparation complete, our project is ready to get started. Finally, this many pages in, we're going to talk about project management itself - strap in, it's going to be fast and bumpy ride!

STRUCTURE PROVIDES THE FOUNDATION FOR YOUR FREEDOM TO ACT

5: HOW DO WE MANAGE A PROJECT?

So, we've covered everything that happens before we do anything. And our sights turn to actually doing project management!

Earlier we discussed how we need to move from a state of *Ready-Fire-Aim* to *Ready-Aim-Fire*.

To do that, takes structure.

An HR Project Management Protocol

There are those that believe that removing all limitations is the primary route to creativity and freedom to act. They say that when we are at liberty to do anything, our effervescent minds will spiral into new galaxies of inventiveness and audacious confidence.

Except...

It's not true. Time after time after time, it is proven that ingenuity, creativity and innovation require limitations and boundaries.

Put simply, despite a million well-intended memes and training courses, in order to think outside the box, we first *must have a box!*

In a very similar way, there are those who believe that having structure to work will stifle performance, flexibility and responsiveness to shifting business environments. Better to shoot from the hip and keep moving than slow down to consider next steps.

And, of course, there's always a balance.

But, as we've seen up to this point, HR has a great way of avoiding change by keeping things in the intuitive space. And, when it comes to projects, that is a *major* problem.

So, if we are to adopt a project management mindset and discipline, we must be prepared to shift our view of structure.

Project success rests upon the structure we put in place, and our commitment to hold to it

So, let's turn our attention to a structure that has been proven successful time upon time: a simple 4-stage *HR Project Management Protocol.*

This can be summarized as *"Scope it, Plan it, Deliver it, End it"* as shown in the graphic on the next page.

In the next four chapters, we'll cover each stage in detail, then we'll move on for a closer look at managing stakeholders.

HR PROJECT MANAGEMENT PROTOCOL

INITIATE	**SCOPE THE PROJECT**
PREPARE	**PLAN THE PROJECT**
IMPLEMENT	**DELIVER THE PROJECT**
COMPLETE	**END THE PROJECT**

hrprojmgmt.com

6: INITIATE THE PROJECT

In this phase, we detail the business case for action, outcomes we expect to achieve, resource we plan to deploy, and how we intend to deliver.

Before we get specific, be aware that it's OK to not have all the answers before we get going. You'll see in the next few sections that we're going to estimate some things based upon best guess, that we'll only be able to flesh out with specifics once we're underway.

But now, drum roll please, welcome to THE most important tool you will use in delivering your project.

Project Charter

The Project Charter is a structured document with two-fold purpose. Firstly, we use it to capture key information about the project intent, charting the roadmap to success; and, secondly, we use it to engage key stakeholders sufficiently to authorize the project.

PROJECT CHARTER TEMPLATE

Mandate/Business Need

Why must we do this project?

Deliverables

What will the project make happen?

Project Completion Criteria

How will we know the project has delivered its remit?

Business Value Measures

What is impacted? (Time, Cost, Quality)

Project Resources

Who will manage the project? Who will do the work of the project? Who will provide subject matter input and reaction to the project team?

Functional Intersections

Where will the project touch other functions, processes and systems?

Initial Planning

What are the high-level timeline and key milestones for the project?

hrprojmgmt.com

Let's take a look at each of these sections in more detail.

Detailing the business case

Describing the Mandate/Need

The first thing we look at here is to vividly describe the mandate/need. This can be as long or as short as it takes to adequately state the *"Why?"* of the project.

A well structured mandate/need can be tested for quality based upon 4 dimensions (score each 1-10):

- Bottom line impact? (WHY are we doing this?)
- Context for deliverables/milestones (WHAT will be happening?)

- Stakeholder frame-of-reference (WHO will be affected, and HOW?)
- Source for *"Elevator Speech"*? (HOW will we describe the business case?)

If you scored less than 25, then don't go any further... Knowing, and being able to fully articulate the mandate/need is *essential* to running a successful project, especially in HR where, as we've discussed, so many projects emerge from best intent around pain points.

A great business case combines FACTS and FEELINGS to justify going forward. Keep re-working it until you score at least 35 in aggregate across all 4 criteria.

Describing the deliverables

Once we have our mandate/business need stated, we move on to describing our deliverables.

Now, this is one of those areas where we may not know the absolute final shape of things - for example, if our project is to design and build a new employee-facing system, at some point in the project we are likely to review and assess potential software vendors. That's fine and understandable.

In our charter, we would describe the deliverable as something along the lines of: *"Assess, validate and approve any final software solution"*.

Once again, we don't need to have all the answers to begin to lay out our deliverables roadmap.

Describing Project Completion Criteria

At this stage, we'll also begin to lay out some forward looking expectations in the form of Project Completion Criteria. Note that these criteria are about delivering the project, not the ultimate deliverable in the business, which we'll get to in a moment.

My own favorite way of describing this to stakeholders is simply, *"How will we know we've done a great job?"*

So, in the case of our software system, we might have a completion criteria that *"System support and training options in place and being utilized by end users"*.

Actually, I should note that this is actually 3 completion criteria in one! 1) System support; 2) Training Options; 3) Use of support and training.

In this example, we're not saying how, or by when, or who will deliver. We're simply saying that we'll know we've done a great job when people are able to use our solution. Importantly, we're not saying what users will actually accomplish by using the system. For Project Completion Criteria, we can consider ourselves effectively blind to outcomes.

Note that this is just one of what is likely to be several completion criteria - be careful of going too overboard - and, especially, watch that you don't extend completion criteria beyond the scope of the project.

For example, while we may have a project completion criteria to put in place a new annual bonus process by December of the current year, we would not claim that the project will only be successful when next year' gross revenue increases by 15% thanks to all the wonderful motivation the bonus will create; we may hope that the new annual bonus may contribute to that level of growth but it's outside the project scope!

Describing Business Value Measures

Which brings us neatly to the final piece of our business case: *Business Value Measures*.

These are the outcomes of the project in the business.

As a data-fiend, I'll be the first to express my frustration about the availability of valid, tangible Business Value Measures. This isn't always an easy matter for HR projects, because so many things associated with our function are measured in the aggregate, if they're measured at all!

For example, let's say we have a project to redesign the corporate recruitment gateway. What are the best business value measures?

Is it *time-to-hire? Cost-per-hire? Hiring Manager satisfaction? Candidate engagement? 1st year retention? Recruitment source metrics?*

Any or all of those may be touched/affected by our system - but that doesn't make all of them candidates for our project Business Value Measures.

If anything, in this particular example, we would do well to look towards more online user activity analytics such as user retention, page drill-downs, etc.

Whatever we choose to measure, it is essential at this stage that a baseline can be measured! If we are going to want to measure improvement in metric A in 12 months time, and attribute improvement to our project deliverables, then we'd better have a really, really clear picture of what metric A says today and, preferably, it's historical value over time.

Estimating project resources

Now, this is where things begin to get even fuzzier. We are, after all, predicting how much resource will be required to deliver a project when we haven't yet generated a plan or timeline...

Fear not, there's no need to reach for a crystal ball! Remember, we've reserved the luxury of using our best-guess estimate at this stage. The next phase of the protocol (PREPARE) will go much deeper, and provide much greater granularity on tasks and timelines. For now though, consider that you're starting every sentence with *"Based on what I know so far, I think that…"*

Before you grab this as a *get-out-of-jail-free* card, I have to let you know that we can't leave this completely open. If we are going to engage stakeholders around the project - and, of course, we are - then we have to at least be in the ball park.

My preferred route to estimating project resources is to break it down into the following, using Full-Time Equivalents (FTE) for forecasting. Though not an exact science, it does get us a surprisingly long way to being able to say *"this is what it's going to take to get this done…"*

Let's take a look at how this approach to best-guess estimation works.

There are 3 broad categories of people that will be assigned to projects: Full-time, Part-time, and Subject Matter Experts.

Here's how I define each category, and how I handle them when estimating resources.

Full-time Resources

People who will be dedicated 100% to the project (1 FTE per person)

Part-time Resources

Estimate how many team members will regularly give time to the project and calculate time expectation for each person (e.g. 1 morning of a 5-day work week is roughly 0.2 FTEs)

Subject Matter Experts

Though it's difficult to estimate subject matter expertise for every project, it can be useful for certain work. For example, for a global process design project, it would be appropriate to estimate that a process specialist might give two hours per week for 4 weeks when their process is on the chopping block (if you really want to, you can calculate the FTEs, though the temporary nature of the assignment makes it an exercise in unnecessary detail!)

The bottom line is that it's easier to forecast people who are 100% assigned to the project but, as we all know, most HR projects don't get that luxury.

So, at this stage, our forecast estimate might look something like this:

	Number of people	FTE per person	Total FTEs
Project Manager	1 Person	0.5 FTE	0.5 FTE
Project Core Team	4 People	0.2 FTE	0.8 FTE
Subject Matter Experts	10 People	0.05 FTE	0.5 FTE
		TOTAL	**1.8 FTEs**

And, of course, it's not absolute but even this estimate tells me that, for the lifetime of the project, we're going to be applying about 2 people's worth of resource to getting it done.

A brief aside on contracted resource, which may come into discussions here. If any of these roles is to be provided by a contractor, then it still counts as resource, though the cost must be added to the project budget.

As an aside, I'm not going to cover budgeting in great detail in this book for a couple of reasons: 1) Nearly every CHRO I've discussed the subject with talks about delivering projects with nil-budget using majority of in-house resources on part-time project membership basis; and 2) Financial norms and rules differ from company to company and even from department to department within companies. Needless to say, if you have to forecast a budget for your project, use your best guess and allow for a budget overspend - from construction and remodeling projects, it seems that 25-30% overspend is a reasonable expectation.

As we discussed earlier, forecasting project resources helps HR leadership make decisions about how they want to backfill any people deployed to the project.

In our example above, we need to look at what happens to the Project Manager's regular work while the project is running, and also what work can be delayed or reassigned to free up a morning or afternoon a week for the project core team members.

Providing an initial timeline

We've already looked at why it's essential to have a Project Manager with credibility in the HR function and beyond, and important that is for stakeholder engagement, and ensuring the likely traction of project deliverables.

But equally important is that for our charter we have to be able to estimate how long it takes to get something done. And that takes somebody with insight and experience of the subject matter of the project.

For example, I can tell you how long it takes to prepare, deploy, analyze and report out the results of an employee engagement survey. Because I've managed such projects enough times to know what to expect.

Similarly, a credible Project Manager in the Compensation space will be able to tell you what it takes to design, communicate and implement a new performance-related bonus.

So, assuming we have a Project Manager who knows what they're talking about, how deep should the initial planning go in our charter?

The answer is, of course, *"it depends…"*

If the project is surrounded by stakeholders who are likely to be resistant and/or skeptical about the project's likely success, then it's better to err on the side of key milestones (e.g. *"Performance payments available in system, September 1st"*) than more specific activities (e.g. *"Review and reduce colleague eligibility criteria for performance payments"*) so that you minimize the likelihood of setting off alarm bells, and thereby providing easy hooks for knee-jerk resistance.

That said… It depends!

Because you may work in an organization culture that values and promotes specificity and courageous conversations, and that culture may demand that tough reality is highlighted early and with complete transparency.

I have to say that, even though I've come across organizations that claim this, I have yet to find one that demands such standards across all behavior and activity - I want to believe that's out there somewhere, but I'm not holding my breath…

If it is the case though, be as specific as you need to be to reduce the impact of *"land-mines"*.

Identifying the team

Do you need to have a project core team? Well, the answer is a highly qualified *"maybe…"*

Basically, we have need of a project team when the work of the project is bigger than one person. It really is that simple. But that doesn't help has identify who should be on the core team.

So, let's take a look at some of the reasons for considering core team membership for a given project, some of which seem contrary to our earlier discussions.

Project Manager focus

The primary reason for considering additional resources on a core team is that of freeing Project Manager focus. Put bluntly, you don't want your Project Manager distracted from managing the project, and this can happen rapidly if your Project Manager is only assigned to the project part-time - whether alongside their regular day job, or because they are handling many of the project tasks directly. Either way, risk creeps into the project when the Project Manager isn't able to focus fully on their core accountability of managing the work.

Subject matter expertise

Once again, this is a matter of freeing up the Project Manager. We spent some time earlier discussing the fact that it's not always a good idea to ask a Subject Matter Expert to manage the project. And that discussion is all still valid. However, if there is an individual who knows the subject inside out, and/or who handles the content every day, it makes absolute sense to consider them for the core team, as they will be likely to help move project work faster and with greater focus.

Professional development

Being directly involved in a project is a great way for an up-and-coming HR professional to see how the wider function works, including processes, governance, systems and organization culture. Depending on the person, it may also be a way to begin the process of building project management capability, by pairing up the junior resource with a more seasoned Project Manager. As with all development opportunities, this works best when it is part of a structured growth plan, with clearly defined expectations and outcomes.

And, just so I said it, please don't use projects as dumping grounds for poor performers.

Key representation

We've talked at length about the pathology of HR when it comes to involving people in projects to protect against project deliverables. That all still stands as discussed, however…

There are times when it's necessary to involve a member of a potentially-highly-resistant faction in the project team.

There, I said it. Sometimes you do have to *"invite the enemy in"*.

This is particularly the case for projects emanating from Centers of Expertise, where the output of the project reaches directly into the business, touching leaders, managers, or individual contributors - but where front-line HR Business Partners are not directly involved.

For example, one of my most successful projects was a global HR process redesign ready for migration to an online system, and we flipped things over so that the core team was completely staffed by HR Business Partners. We made a great team, and we ended up involving a many other HR Business Partners as SMEs on a rolling basis. We completed the task early, at reduced budget and to popular reception across the function - a result that can be directly attributed to the fact that, by design, the project touched almost 30% of the function at some point.

There is a simple bottom line here:

INVOLVE ONLY THOSE PEOPLE IN THE
PROJECT WHO ARE READY, WILLING
AND ABLE TO MOVE THE PROJECT
FORWARD

The importance of beginning well

In this chapter, we've covered what, for me, is the most important aspect of any project: *beginning well.*

And yes, it's always possible to catch-up once the project is running - and you'll undoubtedly meet situations where you have to do just that - but an ounce of prevention is better than any amount of the cure.

But that's not really the point of beginning well. When we initiate the project using a robust Project Charter, we stick a flag in the sand and state clearly: *"we intend to do this!"*

As we know, all humans prefer to belong to something than to be cast adrift. Last I checked, I and other members of HR are like, totally, human... While our shape and flavor of projects may be different, we are not. So beginning well takes that spirit even further.

Our flag in the sand now states: *"I am part of doing this!"*

Why is such ownership important? Well, in the regular course of events, it's good for getting things done. But when the project hits a rough patch - and it will either due to practical circumstances, or due to the self-sabotage we've discussed throughout this book - ownership of the project becomes critical. It's just too easy to abandon ship, either literally or figuratively, when the going gets tough; ownership provides a significant hedge against that risk.

As we close this chapter, I have to say that I've not witnessed too many flame-outs when it comes to projects or Project Managers. But I have seen projects left to wither on the vine, just limping along like an old and tired 3-legged dog. It's a shame for the Project Manager and the business as a whole.

Those projects that succeed know the trick: *begin well to end better.*

And that brings us, to paraphrase Winston Churchill, to the end of the beginning!

Let's move on to PREPARING THE PROJECT!

7: PREPARE THE PROJECT

And so, finally, we arrive at what most people think project management is.

Thanks to widespread use of Microsoft Project and similar software packages way back before online and app options were even a thing, ask anyone to draw you a project plan, and you'll get a Gantt chart, a series of blocks, diamonds and arrows flowing left-to-right, top-to-bottom. Something like this:

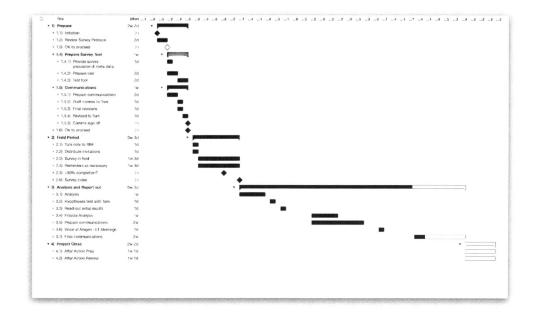

To those of us who run projects, project timelines such as Gantt are everyday normality - it's just how the world works.

It took me several years running projects in HR, however, before I learned that, surprisingly often, such views of project plan, progress and anticipation aren't always understood, or favored, by key stakeholders in HR.

So, a little later on in this chapter, we're going to talk about alternatives.

For now, though, I'll talk to the Gantt because it makes sense and, for Project Managers, is the accepted standard view of plan - and, if you want to build transferable skills, Gantt is your bread and butter!

3 core building blocks

For the purposes of HR projects, a plan consists of 3 basic building blocks: *Tasks*, *Milestones*, and *Decisions*.

Now, strictly speaking, a Decision can look like a Task, and it can be marked by a Milestone, but I call it out separately here because it is so very, very important to keep an eye on decisions in HR projects - for all the reasons of self-sabotage we discussed earlier.

Let's look at each building block.

Tasks

A task is a piece of work - it receives an input, has an output, takes a finite amount of time and resource to get done.

On a Gantt chart, a task is captured as its own row, and symbolized by a rectangular bar.

The width of the task rectangle corresponds to time - i.e. how long it is planned to take to get done.

If a task receives input from a previous task, it will be linked by an arrow - called a *Dependency* in project management terminology.

Most project software will also let you indicate to which resource the task is assigned.

Here's an example of four tasks in a very simple project plan:

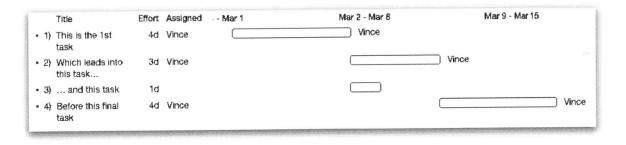

As you can see, tasks 2 and 3 can't be completed before task 1 is done. And, in turn both must be completed before task 4 can be started.

This view also shows assigned resource per task and, aside from the fact that I seem to be carrying a lot of the weight(!), task 3 is not currently assigned to anyone; it also has some flexibility around when it actually needs to be done in those 3 days that task 2 is happening.

This is a really quick and easy example of how a Gantt chart can highlight ambiguities and flex within a project plan.

Later we're going to be talking about approaches to planning, many of which are driven by preference - if the Project Manager for this project is of the opinion and preference that last-minute deadline driven planning is the right thing, then this project plan might look more like this:

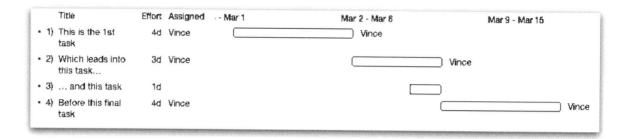

Do you see the difference? Once you get used to working with Gantt charts, they quickly become a) simple to use; and b) indispensable in planning!

Milestones

So, we know how to plan for tasks in our project plan. A *Milestone* is a different beast, but straight-forward to understand and represent.

A Milestone is, as its name suggest, a specific point on the journey. It tells us that an outcome has been achieved, an output delivered, an external deadline imposed, or a decision reached.

On a Gantt chart, a Milestone is represented by a diamond shape - and, depending on the software you choose, it might also be considered a task of 0 time duration.

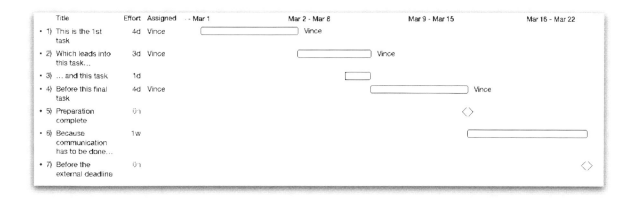

Title	Effort	Assigned	- Mar 1	Mar 2 - Mar 8	Mar 9 - Mar 15	Mar 16 - Mar 22
• 1) This is the 1st task	4d	Vince	⬜ Vince			
• 2) Which leads into this task...	3d	Vince		⬜ Vince		
• 3) ... and this task	1d			⬜		
• 4) Before this final task	4d	Vince			⬜ Vince	
• 5) Preparation complete	0n				◇	
• 6) Because communication has to be done...	1w					⬜
• 7) Before the external deadline	0n					◇

Let's extend our example project plan to include some specific milestones, that signify the completion of tasks.

Here, we can see a *"Preparation complete"* Milestone 5 (an outcome) after task 4, which then enables task 6 (communication) to occur before the external deadline, marked by the final Milestone 7.

Once again, we'll be looking at approaches to planning in a little while but, using our example, there are a couple of ways to think about milestones:

a) *"When will the preparation work be complete so that we can start communicating?"*; or...

b) *"In order to deliver on the deadline, when do we need to start communicating? And what do we need to do to be ready for that?"*

These are talking about the same events, but a) is looking from the present-forward, while b) is looking from the future-back.

As I say, stay tuned, because that's a critical distinction in terms of planning the project.

Decisions

As I mentioned earlier, in most projects, *Decisions* are treated as any other Milestone, that is as a point in time event or checkpoint.

For HR projects though, particularly those that are likely to cause significant downstream change, I will often take the luxury of calling out Decisions, and decision prep, as a class all on their own.

Diagrammatically there isn't that much difference. It's still a matter of rectangles and diamonds, but I use color to highlight where critical decisions are expected - though they'll print in shades of grey here.

In our plan, for example:

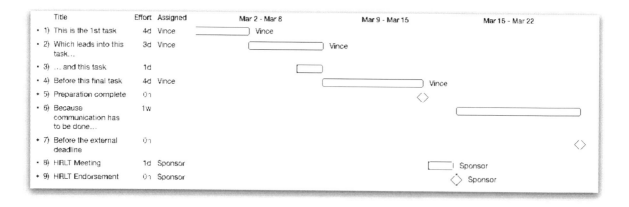

In this project plan, we've now added a necessary decision gate for HR Leadership Team review and endorsement. Using the colors yellow for task 8 and red for decision 9 make these events stand out, and very quickly draw attention. You'll also note that I've assigned these tasks to the Project Sponsor.

From a timeline perspective, there is an argument to move 8 and 9 above 6 to continue the sequential time flow. That's really a matter of preference and style. Mostly, I would move these into a sequence, however if a project is sensitive and requiring a ton of change readiness work, it can help to keep all such actions in one horizontal section, so that there is clear visibility of the integrated change management work across the project.

Of course, the beauty of using a software solution is that you can choose your own approach based upon the audience for the plan - your Project Team may prefer linear, when your Sponsor and other Key Stakeholders may prefer things in groups.

That said, be careful of running too many plan formats - it can be a nightmare to keep everything updated across formats and presentations - and software solutions generally don't do well with taking a single data set and automatically rendering it to alternative views - there's always tweaking to do.

Approaches to planning

So, we've covered the 3 building blocks of a project plan: *Tasks, Milestones* and *Decisions*.

The real trick to planning is not the blocks, as much as it is how we choose to lay them out.

It would be nice to say that there is a prescriptive approach to planning - one-size-fits-all would make this section so much easier to write - but it really does come down to personal preference.

But no matter what, we always start with the business case described in the Project Charter - the unique product or service the project will deliver.

We're now able to put in our first milestone at some point in the future: *"Unique Product or Service Delivered"*.

Now, this milestone may be considered *"soft"* or *"hard"*.

A *"soft"* milestone is one where we don't know what date the milestone will be due, and most HR project planning will begin with a *"soft"* milestone - i.e. *"we know something will happen, but we're not sure when..."*

It should be pretty obvious that a *"hard"* milestone is one where we know specifically what date the milestone will be delivered. Examples might include benefits enrollment where there is a calendar deadline for completion, performance-related bonus with a year-end payment, etc.

Either way, have some idea of when we'll end up being done!

The preference comes with how we chart the path to get there. There are two main flavors of approach.

Future-Back Planning

The essence of Future-Back Planning is to start with the end in mind. We take our final milestone and take a step back towards the present to find the predecessor milestone. Once we have that, we step back and find the previous one, and so on, and so on, until we arrive back to the present day.

Present-Forward Planning

Present-Forward planning starts with where we are today, figures out what is missing, then plans the work to put it in place. So, for our example of a performance-related bonus, we would say that there needs to be a process for deciding who gets it, communication materials, a bonus fund, etc. Then we'd stage those pieces of work into a reasonable flow so that we'd be ready to deliver by end-of-year.

With all of our milestones identified, we then flood the plan with the activities to achieve each milestone, including the estimated duration and resource.

Add in dependencies - i.e. what has to be in place before we can move forward on each activity, and the plan begins to assemble itself.

Same building blocks, just a different approach to planning.

And both come with risks from blind spots.

Future-Back Planning risks myopic focus on only those things that will deliver the project, because we are asking questions in a thin channel towards a specific deliverable.

Present-Forward Planning risks an inefficient plan, simply because we are basing things on previous experience. If it's always taken us 7 weeks to generate, refine and approve a policy statement, then we might automatically put 7 weeks on our plan.

Neither approach is right nor wrong, it really does come down to the Project Manager's preference - so pick one and manage to it

That said, I have to say that one of the places HR projects grind to a halt is by diving into the weeds of tactics. At this stage of planning, it's essential that the Project Manager avoids this descent to make sure things stay on track.

Remember, PLANNING THE PROJECT is not DOING THE PROJECT - and, like it or not, the project plan will always have to flex once things are underway.

I've found that Future-Back Planning is very helpful in keeping things objective and focused upon results - but then, I would say that, it is my own preference, after all!

Identifying the Critical Path

Whether we use Future-Back or Present-Forward planning, we end up with, at minimum, the milestones we will reach as the project runs. We may also have some idea of time and resource it will take to deliver those milestones.

It's worth pausing here to talk about Critical Path Analysis, which will become of increasing importance the more complex your project plan.

Basically, the Critical Path of a project is made up of things that MUST happen before the next thing can happen.

Typically, we'll find key governance decisions on the Critical Path, along with key project deliverables.

By way of illustration, let's say we're running a project to deliver an employee survey. Before we can launch the survey, we must have a ratified list of employees and their emails (project deliverable), and we must have a formalized decision whether paper surveys will be available (governance decision).

If it takes 4 weeks to produce a ratified list of employees, and our decision to have paper surveys adds 3 weeks printing and distribution, along with 5 weeks collection and transcription into the reporting system, then we have just added 12 weeks to our Critical Path.

Once again, we have a preference on when we use Critical Path - once we've developed the whole plan, to identify bottlenecks, etc. or starting from the Critical Path and working outwards.

As I mentioned earlier, my preference is Future-Back planning, and I have to admit that my first cut of a project plan looks like only those milestones and decisions that would lie on the Critical Path. This gives me a very early view of the best case scenario of project timeline - i.e. any task, milestone, or decision that's added only has the potential to slow things down.

But, as I say, that's my preference, it might not work for you if you're a more granular Present-Forward type of Project Manager.

One word of caution here, though. Many project planning tools offer an automated Critical Path Analysis tool, which can be very useful *if you have a detailed plan in the tool*. Be careful, however, of taking its output as absolute - always review with a critical eye - while this may be the case with everything software-related, it does seem especially prevalent in project management software.

Big Asks vs. Quick-N-Easy

An early Critical Path Analysis can identify bottlenecks in terms of time and resource, and the timing/sequencing of critical decisions.

Even before we get to specific planning of task, time and resource, you should have an eye open for what is likely to be considered a BIG ASK - as in, the project is going to ask someone, or some group, to do something that will take significant time, resource, focus, or change.

I like to think of BIG ASKS as those moments in a project where I might find myself losing sleep, or where going into a meeting feels like preparing for battle.

For example, when I was asked to lead a project to redesign the global Organization Development function and service delivery model, one of the critical milestones was our presentation to the HR Leadership Team of initial findings and prototype model. I had presented to that team many times, and knew its strengths and weaknesses, and where I'd had *"hits"* and *"misses"*. Thanks to that experience, and the then-state of HR Transformation, I knew that it would be a tough conversation, no matter what shape our prototype took.

As a result, that meeting and its prep were colored bright red on the plan, so that we kept an eye on them at all times. Identification of this BIG ASK early let us pressure test all our work with a view to how it fed towards that critical meeting.

And, because honesty and transparency is important to me, I have to tell you that - despite the best intentions, actions, and decisions of the project team - that meeting did NOT go well. Win some, lose some, and always keep learning...

On the flip-side to the BIG ASK is the Quick-n-Easy - those items that are on the Critical Path, but we have full confidence we can deliver to plan. If these are so easy, why do we look for them upfront? The answer is simple, though the Quick-n-Easy items may be critical, we can pay less attention to them than we do their cousins, the BIG ASK items.

Downplay a Critical Path item?! You bet, put it in monitor mode, so you don't obsess over it - save your obsession for the BIG ASKs!

Said differently, it's really important to keep objective perspective on your project plan and this starts long before we actually do a single thing.

Built to flex

Inevitably, we end up at the question: *how detailed does the plan need to be?*

And the answer is two-fold. Firstly, it needs to be detailed enough for the Project Manager to keep the train on the tracks throughout implementation. Secondly, it needs to be detailed enough to inform key stakeholders throughout implementation.

Now, the first part of that should make absolute sense.

The second part is a more fuzzy because, while you want key stakeholders informed, does it really take a fully detailed plan to do so?

When it comes to project plans and stakeholders, being known to have one is almost as important as what the plan itself says. You see, if you get the sponsorship and Project Manager selection right, you already have a reservoir of trust and credibility associated with the project. So stakeholders will give the benefit of the doubt with respect to the plan.

Until the rubber hits the road, and things begin to happen, of course... then they'll want reassurance that what they're seeing isn't random, chaotic stuff...

And, just like that, we're back in the land of self-sabotage.

Essentially, your plan has to be able to answer a number of questions at any point in time - *What is happening? Why is it happening now? What does it mean? What's going to happen next?* If it can't, then that reservoir of trust and credibility will leak away pretty quickly.

So, the answer to our original question of how detailed the plan should be is: detailed enough to deliver objectives, withstand challenge and reassure stakeholders.

And there is one really, really important caveat here. In any and all conversations relating to the plan, be sure to reinforce the fact that *"this is the plan as it stands right now"* and that you fully expect the plan to be adjusted as action, events and decisions occur.

Essentially, all project plans are built to flex. So make sure you educate people of that fact!

Personally, my preference is to always send the latest plan to PDF for distribution, printing, or online archive, with a footnote along the following lines:

"This plan represents <name of project> project outlook as of <insert date here> and is considered archived. Please contact <Project Manager> if you have any questions as to current status"

This, along with tight version control of documents, can help stave off many opportunities for self-sabotage to rear its head.

Before we move on from building your plan, let's quickly cover a risk that might arise, depending on your preferences.

When it comes to planning, and particularly with respect to project management software, be very careful of falling down the rabbit-hole of designing the perfect project plan. Just as with Powerpoint, Word, or any other software solution, you can end up in formatting craziness and, when added to a preference to detail every last action down to what feels like a by-the-minute snapshot, things can quickly grind to a halt.

Bottom line: Your job is not to deliver the perfect project plan, it's to deliver the project. Forecast enough detail to get things done, and make it presentable. Then manage the project!

A Gantt Chart or a Calendar?

Well, we've covered a lot of ground in this chapter, most of which is focused on the planning before the doing. In the next chapter, we'll be moving on to the doing - finally, GETTING THINGS DONE!

But, before we do, there's one more heads-up that I want to share.

I've written a lot in this chapter about Gantt charts, and how to represent and organize our 3 building blocks: *Tasks, Milestones,* and *Decisions*. There's very little I love more in a project than a well-designed, useful, and focused Gantt chart. In the right hands, they can be something of a work of beauty.

However…

I learned very early on in my project management experience, that many people in HR, and especially HR leaders, *just don't get* Gantt charts. Time and again in those early days, the project team would share the Gantt chart with members of HR, only to then field really basic questions about if and/or when certain tasks would be happening.

Sometimes, these were dressed up in *"Have you thought about…"*, which is a subtle self-sabotage game that gets played. But more often, it was clear that members of HR just couldn't make sense of that left-to-right cascading timeline.

And, even worse, members of HR who couldn't make sense of a Gantt chart were being asked to lead projects and then producing their own Gantt charts for other people to be confused by. It was Gantt madness!

My epiphany came while preparing for a particular HR leadership team meeting, when the Project Sponsor mentioned a recent conversation with an HR leader who had asked when a certain task would be happening.

When I confirmed the date, and that it hadn't changed in any iteration of the plan, our Sponsor asked whether we'd communicated it to the HR leadership team, because the *HR leader didn't see it on their calendar…*

The lightning bolt struck. I took a gamble and rendered the project plan in calendar format - most project management software will do this, though it's not always pretty, so be prepared to edit - highlighting the critical actions and decisions expected of the HR leadership team. I distributed both the calendar and Gantt version of the project plan, with a note that the calendar view was to help their own planning.

I also forwarded the calendar view to their Executive Assistants to get the key items on their calendars.

My insight was simple but powerful. When we are managing a project, the detail of the project is in our conscious mind all the time. Others are dealing with their own world, and our project is quite often an intrusion. For that reason, we need to help the project to speak in the language/format that works for our stakeholders.

We'll talk about this in more detail when get to the chapter on stakeholder management, but for now, be ready to produce a calendar and/or event view to go alongside your Gantt chart.

From our example project plan:

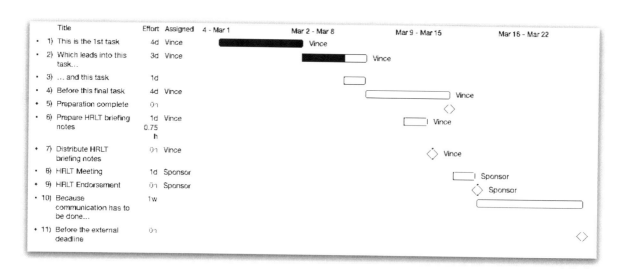

My calendar view would literally show tasks 8) and 9), i.e. *"at this meeting, we will seek your endorsement"*, though I wouldn't word it quite like that.

As you can see, I've also inserted two items: 6) An activity to produce briefing notes for the HRLT; and 7) A milestone to distribute the briefing notes. These extra tasks would likely not be shown on the calendar view, as they relate to internal project work. Wherever possible, I would aim to deliver those briefing notes in whatever meeting-prep rhythm already existed for the HRLT. If this were an off-rhythm meeting, however, I would indicate Milestone 7) on the calendar (i.e. *"we will send you briefing notes on… ahead of the meeting on…"*).

Onboarding the team

Unless you're a project team of one, it's impossible to talk about *"Preparing the Project"* without covering the activities to bring your project team on-board.

Remember, we've already made sure that the runway is clear, and we've agreed expectations with both the project team member and their manager. So, it's now a matter of moving beyond introductions, and forming your team.

Now, I strongly encourage you to invest in getting to know your team members individually AND as a group.

As people, you need to understand what drives them, and how they thrive to produce their best work.

As a group, particularly if the members haven't worked together before, you're looking for work style preferences and the potential for synergy and/or friction.

You'll have your own techniques and approaches to do this, for sure, so I won't try and provide a one-size-fits-all answer here. I do want to highlight one great way to build immediate working relationships with your team members that is unique to project management.

Involve your team in planning

It's easy for a Project Manager to draw up the plan in isolation - and, sure, that'll practically deliver the tool you need. But for every efficiency gain we make by doing so, we lose the opportunity for buy-in, involvement and, ultimately, ownership of the project by all involved in the project.

Personally, I like to scrum down with team members either individually or, preferably, as a group and work the plan in the room, using Post-It® notes on a wall to sequence the main activities, milestones and decisions, then physically move them around to arrive at the best flow.

Having the team involved in this helps illuminate blindspots, and make connections that we alone may miss.

Another reason to involve the team here is that it can highlight early signs of potential resistance within the team, as well as the attitudes they might be *"transporting"* from those outside of the room. After all, if there's going to be a difference of opinion downstream, it's better to have a heads-up as early as possible.

Wherever possible, in this early involvement, try to be subjectively involved and objectively observing at the same time.

Alongside these specific planning discussions, there is a critical piece of work to be handled at this stage: *formally kicking off the project.*

Let's take a look.

Kicking-off the project

No matter the size of project, I believe a formal Kick-off is imperative, even if work is already underway on project planning and deliverables.

Why is this? Well, one way of thinking about a project is that you're forming a small company - maybe even a start-up - that you need to achieve immediate performance, with little lag-time or grace period. Very, very few companies achieve successful, smooth running in their first year, yet we expect projects to do exactly that in a much shorter time-frame.

For this reason, it's essential that we fast-track classic team formation cycles:

FORM-STORM-NORM-PERFORM

and cut right to PERFORM!

Our aim is to speed up the first three stages: bring people together to a common aim, let them try working together to experience friction points, and arrive at working practices that largely fit the team and individual personalities, styles and approaches.

It's a LOT to collapse, much of which falls upon the shoulders of the Project Manager - particularly the tactical project working structure we've covered earlier in this chapter, which mostly falls under the NORM stage.

So we have to go upstream to the FORMing and STORMing stages and ask the questions: *How do we get everyone involved together, and how do we get them on the same page?*

Which brings us to the Project Kick-off, and the Kick-off Meeting in particular.

Sticking with the small company analogy, we can think of the Kick-off Meeting much as we would a company launch. Thankfully, we're not starting from a blank slate - if we've done everything right to this point, we have all the content we need to flesh out and structure the meeting.

Now, I'm not going to propose a formal, standard agenda template here - the style and approach of such meetings are very much down to organization culture, and what fits in one culture may turn out to be pre-emptive suicide for a project in another.

From our discussion of FORMing and STORMing though, it's pretty clear that there will be some very specific building blocks of our Kick-off Meeting.

1. Everyone directly involved in the project must attend

2. Welcome everyone aboard and reinforce the business intent of the project (Sponsor)

3. Present stakeholder viewpoints and importance (Sponsor and/or guest speakers)

4. Present high-level plan and key stage gates (Project Manager)

5. Discuss working methods and meeting structure (Project Manager)

6. Make clear escalation path for Issues, Risks and Decisions (Project Manager, Sponsor)

7. Set realistic, grounded expectations of involvement and reinforce accountability (Project Manager, Sponsor)

The order and depth of each topic will need to flex, however each of these areas needs to be covered at the outset of the project, otherwise we are choosing to leave landmines and booby traps further down the road.

There is an obvious dovetail between the Kick-off and whatever work may be already happening with core team members, and the planning activity I discussed earlier could be folded into the Kick-off agenda.

I actually prefer not to do that for a couple of reasons.

Firstly, if your Kick-off involves a wider spread of stakeholders, you run the risk of involving them in core team activities, which is one of the aspects of self-sabotage we've already discussed in depth.

Secondly, there's something special about positioning planning discussions as an *"inner circle"* activity, once again we're aiming to increase project team ownership.

As a result, though I do see the two activities as complementary, I don't tend to bring core team tactical work to the Kick-off.

I would draw particular attention to item 5 on the list above, regardless of who attends the meeting, and especially if key stakeholders are invited. That word *"Discuss"* means just that, so be careful that you don't *"talk at"* attendees - remember, this is your opportunity to engage them and gain early warning of potential friction down the road.

As you can probably tell, there is something of a fine line to walk here between involvement/visibility and keeping things within the core team. That's fine, and also part of your learning as to how to position the project with stakeholders.

I highly recommend coupling this content with some form of team developmental assessment such as *Extended DISC, Kolb Learning Styles, Strengthsfinder®,* etc. It doesn't really matter which assessment you choose, so long as it's validated and appropriate, the main aim is to get people into the mindset of STORMing, looking at how preferences and styles may create friction, and then proposing potential working solutions that can be tried and tested - i.e. accelerating towards NORMing.

As an aside, given experience, I have to say that it's a minority of Sponsors who want to be involved in such exercises, sadly, so don't be surprised if they choose to step out to do *"executive-type-stuff"*.

If that happens, though, make sure that this section of the meeting has space for a read-out to the Sponsor of what NORMs are likely to develop. At this stage, it's really important symbolically, strategically and tactically that your Sponsor is seen to be an active participant in the team's process.

And remember, they may be being called in as the first level of escalation should things begin to go off the rails as the project advances, so this serves as a great way of giving them an early heads up.

So, with all that said, we've prepared our project. We have Governance, Charter, Plan, Resources and Team in place; with Sponsor approval, we're good to go.

Time to get things done!

8: IMPLEMENT THE PROJECT

So, the rubber is hitting the road, the train is hitting the tracks and, well… Here's where we make sure nothing hits the fan!

That's right, it's time to manage the project.

And this chapter is going to focus exclusively on the Project Manager because, if the key to developing a project management mindset and discipline in the function is to treat HR projects as if they are projects, then the manifestation of that discipline lies in the habits and practices of the HR Project Manager.

In a moment, we'll dive into these, but before we do, let's just clarify and confirm what I mean by habits; or practices if that makes it easier to internalize. I'm a fan of clean definition, so let's agree that a habit is:

- a settled tendency or usual manner of behavior
- an acquired mode of behavior that has become nearly or completely involuntary

- a behavior pattern acquired by frequent repetition or physiologic exposure that shows itself in regularity or increased facility of performance

Or, said simply, a habit is something you do regularly without thinking about it. Like breathing. Or checking Facebook when a notification pops up. A habit is a practice repeated to the level of unconscious competence.

If anything in this book serves as an operator's manual, it's this chapter. So, if you are a Project Sponsor, or manage an HR Project Manager, you'll want to be monitoring for these beneficial habits. And if you're a Project Manager, trust me, this IS your roadmap.

So, what are the 5 habits of the successful HR Project Manager?

- Own the Plan

- Manage the Work

- Manage the Team

- Involve your Sponsor

- Focus on Stakeholders

What does that mean for the aspiring Project Manager? Well, it means you have to be willing to cycle through *"Conscious Incompetence"* and adopt these habits as planned activities.

So, in a moment, when I talk about owning the plan, it means diarizing 10-15 minutes every morning for a plan review. It'll be the first thing you do in the day, and it will be sacrosanct.

Own the Plan

Manage the Work

Manage the Team

Involve your Sponsor

Focus on Stakeholders

I'll be sure to point out such activities as we go along. For now though, you must commit, and I mean *really* commit, to becoming a better HR Project Manager - it takes full commitment to achieve lasting behavioral change.

So, with all that said, and your commitment in hand, let's dive in.

Own the plan

If you review all our discussions about the Project Plan so far, you will see that we've stuck largely to the technical/functional aspects of planning. We've been talking building blocks, decisions, choices, structure, criticality, etc.

Now that we're underway, however, the plan becomes a living, breathing organism.

If that sounds odd, consider it like this, the plan takes in information, processes it, and puts it out. We could think of this as digestion.

The plan is affected by the world around it, and its own action. We might call this stimulus and response.

The plan interacts with the world via team members, SMEs and associated resources. We might call this the body.

And, if the plan is an organism, then the Project Manager is both the conscious brain AND the beating heart.

How do we keep the plan alive and kicking?

Review the plan often

I mentioned this as a quick example earlier, but let's examine it more deeply now.

The first, and most important, thing is for a Project Manager to know this:

THE PLAN IS ALREADY OUT OF DATE

Remember back when I talked about printing the plan and sharing it with a footer that said as much? Well, that applies equally to our own use of the plan.

So, we have to review, line-by-line to:

- Assess current status
- Forecast activity
- Identify and manage Issues and Risks
- Capture Decisions

We'll go through each of these in detail, but right now let's just focus on the word *"often"*, because you might be asking a question: *How often is often?*

And the answer is, as always, *"it depends…"*

For a short-run project with lots of moving pieces occurring simultaneously, it might be more often than once a day. Though, if that is the case, then it's much more appropriate to run a *"situation room"* type approach, with the project team in one place, receiving status updates and immediately editing the plan live-time. I've done this on a number of global projects - nothing like a project team blitzing a plan via web-meeting - fun, fun, fun!

For a longer-run project, it might be daily or, maybe, as long as weekly, though that begins to build in risk of blind spots.

How often you check the plan also depends on what's happening in the project, and the immediate outlook.

For example, in a global colleague survey, the on-ramp to launch is steady, a lot of data and preparation, but no fireworks. It really is just a matter of getting it done. During this period, I found that personally checking the plan every other day, and supplementing with a weekly team review kept things nicely on track, while not becoming too burdensome.

Fast forward to the week of launch and the field period, and we're all-hands-on-deck - this is when the project is at its most visible and, with a LOT of moving parts, most vulnerable. As Project Manager, it becomes a daily review of status and risks, and on-call availability for issues and trouble-shooting.

So, there isn't a simple, single answer to *"How often is often?"* but I would always err on the side of *"slightly more often than I feel is necessary"*. It should always feel a little like the next project review is one too many, but not so tedious that you begin to skip over details, or make broad assumptions.

A little later, we'll be talking about how to involve your Project Sponsor during this phase; you should review the plan enough that you are ready to answer any question on project status from your Sponsor without having to refer to the plan.

One important reminder here because I can't say it enough:

As a Project Manager, your job is to deliver project outcomes within time, cost and quality criteria - your Project Plan is NOT a project outcome, it is a tool you use to manage project performance. Be careful that you don't spend more time and focus editing the plan than you do managing the project. This is particularly the case if you're using project management software - it can quickly become an exercise in "prettying up the slide" instead of catching the issue and taking action.

So, we've discussed *"How often is often?"* and found that the answer is *"Slightly more often than I feel is necessary?"*

Now let's turn our attention what it means to review the plan, regardless of how often we do it!

Assess current status

The first thing we want to know is *"Where are we, compared to where we thought we would be?"* Or, in other words, an assessment of the current status of the project.

Let's go back to our example plan:

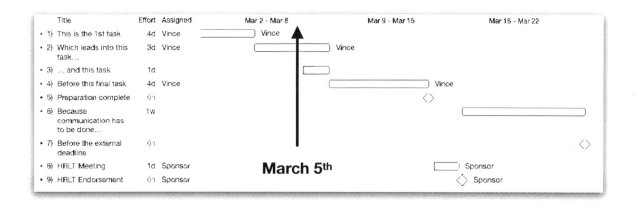

To summarize, in the last chapter we covered how this view represents a number of Tasks leading to 3 consecutive Milestones, one of which is a key Decision.

Now, our timeline is described on a weekly basis in this view - a more granular view might be in days, or even hours. For a long-range project we might zoom out to months, or even quarters.

As you can see, I've indicated March 5th, i.e. heading towards the end of the first week. A quick glance at the plan tells me that Task 1 should be done, Task 2 should be in progress, and Task 3 should be about to start. Now two of these tasks are assigned to some dude called Vince, so my daily check-in is a quick question: *"Hi, Vince - Did you get Task 1 done? And, did you begin Task 2?"*

In a little while we'll talk about *Managing the Team* - and I'll cover how I rarely send such messages when managing a project. But for now, let's keep it here as an illustration of, at minimum, the thought process underlying plan review.

Interestingly, as we review the plan, and notice that Task 3 is about to kick-off, we would also notice that it wasn't assigned to a resource. So, our review question becomes: *"What about Task 3? Who the heck is doing Task 3?!"*

And voila! We've identified a project issue (more about that in a minute).

And that, in a nutshell is how we review current status: *"Where are we, compared to where we thought we'd be?"*

Now, in most project management software there is an option to track current status, including actual vs. planned performance. To do this, we capture a baseline plan in our software.

Let me show you what that might look like for our example project if that guy Vince delivered Task 1 OK, but started Task 2 late, and told us it would take an extra couple of days.

The first thing I do is capture the baseline plan - which is the view above.

I drag the status of Task 1 to *"complete"*, then move and lengthen Task 2.

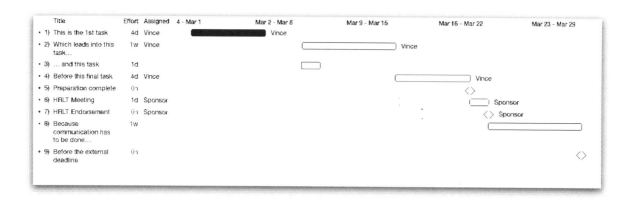

When I now compare the actual (vivid) against the baseline (light), I can immediately see that Vince's delay has pushed our project deliverable out by almost a week - and, of course, I would be making a note that Vince and I need to chat…

The eagle-eyed among you will have noticed that Vince's tardiness didn't affect everything, though. Take a look at Task 3… It hasn't moved! That's because it only relies on the completion of Task 1. So, given that we already have an issue because we don't know who is doing Task 3, we've at least got some wiggle room to find someone, and ask them to get it done, without delaying the project!

Now, I personally love using baseline comparison. It lets me see where the project has been hitting bottlenecks, which I can use as part of my forecasting activity. We'll talk about that in a moment.

For some projects though, where everything runs on time and to plan, I use the completion bar simply to indicate point in time. For example, let's say at March 5th, everything's in progress as planned:

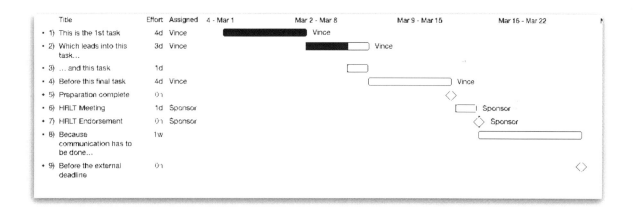

Very quickly, we can see where we're at, so it works for our purposes; if you like Gantt charts, that is… As we've discussed, don't expect this view to work for all HR stakeholders.

In this example, I'm using the completion as a marker of time-passed.

That's not the same as a time-driven project which would use it to track hours spent/used compared to forecast - e.g. *"at this point in time, we've used 60 out of 85 hours scheduled for this task"*.

Or a cost-driven project that would use the completion bar to indicate Resource spent/used compared to budget/forecast - e.g. *"at this point in time, we've used 80% of the consulting dollars set aside for this task."*

Or a quality/performance-driven project that would use the completion bar to indicate widgets produced per task - i.e. *"at this point in time, we have produced 600 of 900 widgets."*

From experience, for the vast majority of HR projects, it is difficult to forecast/ budget resource or productivity to the level of granularity that would facilitate such use of the completion bar - by all means try if you like, but don't end up chasing your tail! Personally, I've found that a simple, point-in-time *"where are we?"* works just fine.

One final note on assessing current status. When we produced our Project Charter, we looked at potential Business Value Measures as part of answering the question *"Why should we do this project?"*

If you were able to gather a baseline, it's always worth keeping an eye on the current data to see if things are changing or even trending while you're running the project.

By doing so, you might see that the business case for your project is getting stronger, or it might be weakening. Either way, you'll be able to respond appropriately.

Depending on the project - if you had a staged roll-out for example - you may be able to see real-time impacts on the measures - it's always useful to be able to see if you're moving the needle at all in either direction.

Manage the work

When it comes to managing the work, everything can be focused in upon how you manage Issues, Risks & Decisions, so let's explore these critical areas.

First, let's define Issues, Risks & Decisions as they pertain to our project.

- An ISSUE is something which IS happening and IS affecting, directly or indirectly, project performance. It can be quantified in terms of Scope, Resources, Timing, and/or Partners. It requires a specific Decision or Action that must be completed.

- A RISK is something which is NOT happening (yet) and which MAY affect, directly or indirectly, project performance. It can be forecast in terms of Scope, Resources, Timing, and/or Partners. It requires a contingency plan that may or may not need to be enacted.

- A DECISION is made by the appropriate stakeholder in order to affect project performance.

You probably read that really quickly, so can I ask you to go back and read it again. It's really, really important.

To boil things down, you have to know that an Issue is not a Risk is not a Decision - they are 3 separate entities. And knowing this is critical to your capability to manage your project.

Issues & Risks

You see, one of the main areas where self-sabotage shows up during HR projects is the mistreatment of RISKS as ISSUES.

143

I've lost count of the number of times a project team or HR stakeholders have gone down the rabbit-hole of *"what happens if…"* when it comes to project deliverables.

Let's look at a simple example of a project with significant personal and political ramifications to illustrate the difference. Say that, in our highly unionized company, our project aims to collapse several legacy pension schemes into one single scheme.

In our example, the project team needs to carry out an assessment of relative numbers of employees on each scheme, and normal expected retirement dates, in order to draw up an initial view of the implementation roadmap.

But let's say that the Compensation Director is concerned what the union reps might say if they knew the project was underway, so is delaying sharing data with the project team.

In this example, the ISSUE is that the project team does not have access to the data it needs to complete the planned assessment.

The RISK is that the unions may react negatively to the outcomes of the project, or even knowledge that the project exists.

In other words, the ISSUE IS happening, the RISK MAY happen.

Note, that doesn't mean the risk is not real nor potentially significant, just that it isn't happening already.

The distinction is important because, right now, the project team can't do very much about the risk, aside from plan a contingency.

And here's the thing, it's not the Union that is slowing things down, it's the Compensation Director.

Ask yourself the question though, if we start talking about potential Union reaction to change with any gathered group of HR professionals, how likely are we to stay focused and keep to a time-limit?

The beauty of clear Issue, Risk & Decision management is that it makes these situations clear and, used wisely, can help us a) avoid the rabbit-holes; and b) focus nebulous concerns into specific, manageable risks.

I use a spreadsheet-based tool for Issues & Risk logging, though some project management software offers online alternatives. One of my main reasons for using spreadsheets is because I can share them easily with HR stakeholders, who aren't always au fait with integrated alternatives!

For our example, in our Issues & Risk Log, we may see something like:

ID	Type	Status	Date Raised	Description of Issue or Risk	Impact	Category	Assigned To	Action Required
						Issues & Risks		
1	Issue	Open	1/1/20	Compensation has not provided data for roadmap assessment	Medium	Change Management	Project Sponsor	Speak with Compensation Director to reinforce project intent and confidentiality.
2	Risk	Open	1/1/20	Union reaction to project intent	High	Change Management	Project Manager	Ensure change management & communication plan includes appropriate involvement of Union reps

and, when reviewing these items at a later project meeting, we might capture:

Action Required	Resolution from	Resolution Date	Decisions Made, Resolution. Contingency Plan
		Resolution	
Speak with Compensation Director to reinforce project intent and confidentiality.	Project Sponsor	1/5/20	Compensation Director released data to project team.
Ensure change management & communication plan includes appropriate involvement of Union reps	Change Management Lead	1/1/20	Change Management Lead is briefed and will plan for involvement and monitor for any interim feedback/reaction

As you can see in the resolution panel, we've addressed the ISSUE that IS happening - the data has been released! - and we've put in place a contingency for the RISK that MAY happen.

Decisions, decisions, decisions

If it's not clear by now, let me state how important it is to stay focused on decisions. Arguably, HR is rooted in decision-science because of our focus on risk management.

As a Project Manager, you're going to get good - *really* good - at the science of managing decisions. Decisions facilitate subsequent progress.

As we've covered earlier in the book, HR will often do anything and everything it can to avoid the finality of a decision. Yet, successful projects thrive on making timely, appropriate decisions.

So decision management comes to the fore because HR has a tendency to debate what's already been discussed to death, as a subtle way to avoid moving forward. We short-circuit this behavioral tic by using a Decision Capture approach and tool.

In some ways, decision capture looks like traditional meeting minutes, though it's a little more specific - by all means fold it into your existing approach, but be sure to specifically detail decisions as described in the tool.

Here's what we're trying to achieve with this approach to decision capture.

What is the decision?

Believe it or not, a simple restatement and confirmation of what has been decided is a) often necessary; and b) highly valuable in actually focusing discussion.

There's nothing quite like sitting in a meeting with a group of key stakeholders, or even just with your Sponsor, after a loooooong discussion and starting a sentence with *"So, we've agreed that…"* before restating the decision. The response

DECISION CAPTURE

Decision Summary

Summarize the decision here

Approval

Who authorized the decision, and on what date? Typically, this will be the Project Manager or Sponsor, although on occasion they may seek further approval from a Key Stakeholder - if that's the case detail this here.

Context

Background

Provide relevant information on the decision here, such as events, previous decisions, need for decision, etc.

Considerations

Considerations are specific factors that informed the decision (e.g. cost-benefit comparison, stakeholder feedback, etc.). They can also be potential down-stream consequences of the decision (e.g. impact on productivity, need to revisit the decision should future events occur, etc.). The main aim of this section is to be able to answer a question further down the road: *"did you think about… ?"*

Document Control

Who captured the decision, on what date. Was the document revised at a subsequent date? If so what changed?

hrprojmgmt.com

is either going to be *"Yes"*, or it's going to be further discussion of the issue at hand; either way we keep going to end until the decision is made.

Our aim here is to confront resistance now, and the first step of naming the decision lays the groundwork. Importantly, this also flushes out passive-aggressive resistance on thorny decisions, and I've found it can help a CHRO hold their HR leaders individually accountable for group decisions.

Who made the decision?

Decisions may need to be revisited, or the fact they were made and agreed might need to be used to call-out subsequent resistance. Either way, we need to capture who was involved in making the decision, and who approved the decision - for those familiar with RACI charting, that would be Responsible(s) and Accountable.

It's much harder to back-track, and even more so to position yourself as an *"outsider"* to project aims, if your name is on the decision capture which you endorsed at the time,

Why did we need to make a decision?

When decisions need to be reviewed and or reconsidered, nobody wants to wade through pages and pages of project notes and meeting minutes, to try and put the rationale back together. Similarly, leaving detail to the vagaries of individual recollection is a major risk, ripe with all manner of biases, and underpinned by our memory of the emotion of the decision-making rather than the substance - i.e. we remember a heated discussion more than the content of that discussion.

So, just as we will see in a moment with Status Reporting, a Project Manager has to be really good at distilling down all of what's gone before into the Background section. Take as much space as you need to capture the rationale.

What did we discuss alongside the decision?

For my money, when it comes to project management in HR, the most important use of the Decision Capture tool lies in documenting considerations. This is, essentially, a capture of how the decision was made, including discussion highlights.

My preference is to bullet areas of discussion during decision-making, including any specific topics or data points, especially if the were considered and denied or put aside. Depending on the project, there might be reason to record these discussions, or use verbatim transcripts - your choice, though I've found summarizing a well-facilitated discussion is sufficient for the vast majority of situations

Why is this so important?

Well, the answer takes us back to our function's favorite pastime: *self-sabotage*.

You see, the game that gets played after decisions have been made is a version of in-the-room *"But what about…"*, and sounds something like *"Interesting, did you think about…"*

And believe me, it's not unusual for this to be asked by stakeholders who were in the room and, know what was discussed - sometimes that's a factor of memory, and sometimes its a play-act of fuzzy memory behind which to hide resistance.

The game is just as it sounds, if I as a resistant stakeholder - conscious or subconscious - can reopen the debate on a decision we are, by definition, not moving forward. So, capturing considerations in the Decision Capture tool provides a hedge against future derailment.

This comes into play particularly when the project hits implementation, because it's relatively easy to sit in a room and decide implementation factors when the project is still in design and development work. And all that can go out of the window as soon as people are affected.

For example, a project that aims to collapse multiple legacy pension plans into a single plan going forward may decide early on that all existing employees are *"grand-fathered"* into the new plan, and that all new employees automatically join the new plan.

At the design stage, we may uncover the fact that the rules for early retirement in the new plan aren't quite as generous as in a subset of the legacy plans. As a result, we may agree, and decide, that business needs demand this, and therefore new plan rules will apply for all members, legacy or otherwise.

Fast forward to the new plan being launched, and the first rumblings of revolt start emerging because people who were already aiming at early retirement are realizing they're losing some benefits. As some of those people are senior executives, who are leaning hard on their HR reps to create an exception just for them.

And hence, the Project Manager and Sponsor are summoned to an ad-hoc HR Leadership Team meeting where the lead HR Business Partner lines up the cross-hairs, turns off the safety lock, and asks *"Did you think about…"*

How does that conversation go if you're trying to remember what was discussed at a meeting months earlier? If you're anything like me, your stomach just sank a little…

How does it go if you are able to pull the specific Decision Capture on *"How to treat early retirees"* whose benefits were being affected by plan migration?

And what if that document indicated that, not only had you discussed it, but the lead HR Business Partner had agreed to take the lead on change management in regard to senior executives who might be affected?

Where might the discussion then go, and what might be the result? Would we cover old ground, or would we stay focused on the current issue?

This example is exactly why we capture decisions and detail considerations.

What's done is done

The final section of the Decision Capture looks kind of admin-ish: *document control*. I mean, surely this is just dating the document and naming the author, right?

Well, not quite. You see, I've yet to meet a decision that was considered so made that it couldn't be revisited and/or remade - this is the real world, after all.

To extend our example above, maybe there's a rich discussion of whether we want to change the rules around early retirement to allow for specific exceptional circumstances. As a project manager, your job is to facilitate that discussion and decision - and your Sponsor is on the hook for whatever end result emerges.

Document control allows us to track the evolution of the decision over time. Your Decision Capture gains an addendum, and you move on!

Status Reporting

It's really important to keep everyone involved directly with the project informed of how things are going. As your project grows in size, impact, or reach, this becomes even more critical, especially if you're touching more and more Key Stakeholders. Indeed, once your project reports into a Program Management Office (PMO), this becomes formalized through an expectation of regular read-outs.

Regardless of expectation, however, I believe that *every* project benefits from regular status reporting, because it provides a structure, approach and toolset that forces objectivity, lifting the Project Manager up from the weeds long enough, and high enough, to spot emergent problems that may threaten project delivery.

But the benefits of status reporting don't end there!

When it comes to external stakeholders, it can be very difficult to maintain the right level of focus - more often than not, they're not living the project and aren't up-to-speed with progress. In fact: *it's a safe working assumption to treat each project communication with external stakeholders like a "first touch"*.

So, status reporting - with its use of summaries, quick reference, and traffic light representation - gets the key points across quickly, without the need for either a deep-dive, or regular-world translation.

In summary, status reporting keeps the project on track, with eye-on-the-prize, and it helps position external stakeholders to enable project progress.

How do we do it?

A Status Report is actually quite simple, a summary of our regular project review.

See the graphic for the content of a Status Report template - my preference is to produce these in a Word Processor to facilitate PDF capture and distribution.

The template is pretty explanatory, and captures a single point-in-time. In spirit we're answering a handful of questions: *How are things going? Where are we compared to where we thought we'd be? What's getting in the way? What's coming up next?*

PROJECT STATUS REPORT

Status

Scope (R/Y/G) | Resources (R/Y/G) | Timing (R/Y/G) | Partners (R/Y/G)

Status Description

Explain Status ratings, including any qualitative information.

Deliverables

List any outputs from the project during the status period - include cost, quality, time metrics where possible.

Activity & Achievements

List activity and achievements towards deliverables here - include cost, quality, time metrics where possible.

Issues

List issues, status (R/Y/G) and resolution activity (Not started, In progress, Complete).

Key Decisions

List decisions made (include date and accountable party).

Risks & Contingencies

Describe each risk, risk level and contingency.

5-Week Outlook

List work, milestones and deliverables due in the next 5-week period.

hrprojmgmt.com

Using Red/Yellow/Green (R/Y/G)ratings

We use this rating approach because a) traffic lights are pretty common and standard across the globe! and b) because we want to escalate the project only when necessary.

Believe me, senior stakeholders don't like to see a Red rating and have a conditioned response to demand things be fixed, which is great if you are positioned as their ally in doing so, as your project can only benefit

It's really important to agree standards for R/Y/G up front:

- Red - Action MUST be taken
- Yellow - Project Sponsor is monitoring/managing
- Green - Project Team is monitoring/managing

By rating an aspect GREEN, we're saying to external stakeholders: *"don't worry, the project team has got it in hand…"*

By escalating to YELLOW, we involve the Project Sponsor either for awareness or action.

Only above that do we call a RED - which is really a full halt, either for Project Sponsor intervention, or involvement of wider stakeholders.

Using colors in your status report will help draw your attention to *"hot-spots"* - though this is more of a Program Management technique, when multiple projects report status to a PMO. This is particularly useful when extending the nomenclature to issues as well as overall status - There's nothing quite like reviewing YELLOW and RED issues with your Sponsor to keep both of you on your toes!

Before we move on from status ratings, I wanted to share a cautionary tale.

I once had a senior leader say to his group *"our Status Reports will have no Red ratings"* - his intent was good, that the organization would be so efficient that no Red ever showed-up - what got interpreted was that using Red was professional suicide - pretty soon, many projects were crashing to the ground because of what had been swept under the carpet…

How often to report status?

Well, it's all a matter of choice based upon project team need, speed of progress, and external interest in the project. In the next section, we'll be talking about regular team meetings, and I'll be recommending a weekly standing meeting, this reduces the need to formally report status to the team.

So, the question really becomes one of external stakeholder interest.

Personally, I think weekly, and even bi-weekly, is too often, and the return on time invested significantly diminishes if there isn't substantial change between status reports. Essentially, you can end up caught in a loop of reporting-for-reporting's-sake, which is a waste of everyone's time.

That said, there may be a particularly anxious external stakeholder that needs that level of support - on the rare occasions I've faced that, I've worked with my Project Sponsor to intervene and talk them down off the ledge a little!

Bottom line, report status as often as there is a reasonable amount of status to be reported, and to keep external stakeholders appropriately aware and informed. Be careful to avoid deciding this frequency in a vacuum - make sure you listen to your stakeholders. You want to be known for both hearing and addressing their needs and concerns, and it is an important foundation for both your project and professional success>

For me, this typically works out best on a monthly basis, or even quarterly for longer-term projects.

Manage the team

When I began the work of putting this book together, I spent a lot of time with CHROs in my network to a) pressure-test whether the book might prove useful; and b) listening to the current pain-points symptoms most of them were experiencing with getting projects done in their function.

Guess what pain-point was *numero uno* across the board?

GETTING PEOPLE TO SHOW UP TO PROJECT TEAM MEETINGS!

It seems such a small thing, and it's definitely connected to the self-sabotage we discussed earlier in the book.

For the Project Manager, however, the downstream effects of this behavior can quickly derail the project. Let's look at some of those effects.

Chasing the team

First of all, let's be clear - HR Project Managers are rarely 100% committed to the project. In other words, they already have a job to do, and the project is another thing on the list.

So, when they have to chase project team members to find out a) why they weren't at the meeting; b) the status of their actions; c) the forecast for their planned actions; and d) issues and risks arising, it's pretty easy to see how their project workload has increased exponentially for *no net benefit to the project*!

As you've already read, I'm a strong proponent of capturing key minutes of meetings as a functional tool and attitude, but we have to be careful of the assumption that a team member who is already missing meetings on a regular basis, is staying up to date with minutes - in my experience, the opposite is the case.

So when you add the need to personally debrief meeting content with absent team members, we're just deep in the land of *"this isn't helping…"*

Doing the work

Pity the poor Project Manager, highly committed to delivering the project and keeping things on track.

They know a task is due…

They know the project team member is AWOL…

But the task is due…

What to do but roll up the sleeves and dive in?

This happens way more often than many Project Managers care to admit. And it's just plain wrong.

And, of course, if the Project Manager is also the subject matter expert/owner, this is a) more likely to happen; and b) more likely to damage long-term success of project deliverables.

Reworking the deliverable

There's nothing quite as demoralizing for a Project Manager as a team member who has been AWOL, unresponsive to follow-up, and who then suddenly, out-of-the-blue, delivers on a task they were assigned, with *output that completely misses the mark*.

Back when I was running the Program Management Office for an HR Transformation Initiative, I followed the progress of a process design project at a distance.

The Project Manager, team, sponsor and stakeholders had agreed that just-in-time, in-process education support was the way to go. Think online wizards, help section, float-overs, etc. Easy. Job done.

Only, the learning professional on the team missed meetings, didn't read the minutes and, in response to status requests simply reassured *"everything's on track"*.

With the launch window approaching, the Project Manager suddenly received the *LONG* message detailing the mandatory online training module, optional in-person training, and new colleague orientation content that would support the redesigned process.

Now, in isolation these might have worked, and any learning professional would have been able to claim a value-add. There was nothing but best intent in their misguided output.

Except that the team, sponsor and stakeholders had already nixed that approach as overkill.

Now, to be fair, once things became clear - and let me tell you, for the Project Manager in question, it wasn't an enjoyable call at all - the learning professional completely owned their miss - but guess what… It was the Project Manager who scrambled to get the content together for launch - because they had been paying attention to what was actually needed and agreed, and knew the subject matter inside out.

Thankfully, the solution to all of these issues is simple, though it takes commitment and will to follow through.

Schedule meetings at the outset

I said it was simple, right?

First things first, let me put our Project Kick-off Meeting in the parking lot (we'll talk about it a lot in the next section: *Involve Your Sponsor*).

When you first draw up your project plan, put regular team meetings on as line items, that way you'll catch them in your regular review.

Put them on team member's calendars, including any web- and/or tele-conferencing. Pro-tip: In the online invite, if your scheduling software allows, mark these meetings as *"high priority"* - seems obvious, but few do it, and it can make a major difference to stakeholders who are living calendar-booking to calendar-booking.

My own preference is to have a standing weekly meeting for the duration of the project. Now, that doesn't come from any deep wisdom, or best practice. There's nothing special about the span of 5 business days in terms of standard units of productivity or performance.

I use a week because the world, and particularly HR, seems to organize around weekly events. So, if the world is thinking along the lines of *"It's Thursday, so…"*, who am I to try to steer differently? My number one rule in change management -

if the energy is already flowing fully in one direction, go with it whenever possible!

And, because work swells to fit the allotted time, guess what happens? That's right, your weekly project meeting soon becomes perfect for a week's worth of project happenings.

And so, the cycle of project life continues.

By putting standing meetings on the calendar on a weekly basis, you already significantly increase the chances of project team attendance.

There's one additional tweak I choose to make whenever possible - though, having run a lot of global/virtual projects, it's not always the case. Make sure that the first handful of meetings - at least 4 - occur face-to-face.

Doing so will accelerate the FORMING-STORMING-NORMING-PERFORMING cycle of team development, laying the basis for all interactions that follow in the project, establishing team identity, and building trust for the inevitable *"courageous conversations"*.

Standardize your team meeting

So, we have our standing project meeting, and we've increased the chances of team attendance. The most important thing now is to make the meetings valuable.

That's obvious, right?

Well, hang on a second. Because value is a relative concept.

And a meeting that is valuable for the Project Manager may not be valuable for the project team, or even the project.

How can that be?

The answer is easy. If the Project Manager hasn't done any prep for the meeting, and is using it as a live-time in-depth review of the project plan, the team will quickly learn that they gain little value from the time, so they will increasingly miss the meetings, or be *"absent-in-person"*.

Sadly, such one-way info-flow meetings happen all the time. And they should stop.

If a Project Manager only places attention on project progress when the team gets together, then that Project Manager isn't treating the project like it's a project.

Just a few pages ago, we discussed how a daily plan review is a must. And with that in place, the team meeting focuses much more on matters arising from those reviews: *issues, risks, progress* and *decisions*.

I know it seems trite to say it but, as a Project Manager, you have to use your time for the best of the project! And you may be surprised at how often this seems to be a blind spot.

So, how do I structure my standing project meetings? I'm glad you asked! :)

- Check-in - 5 minutes
- Plan Review - 10 minutes
- Issues, Risks, and Decisions - 20 minutes
- Looking Forward - 10 minutes
- Reflexive Learning - 5 minutes

If I count right, that makes 50 minutes - so an hour more or less with wiggle room. Over time, each section has the potential to grow or shrink based on content, however my experience is that, if the project is well-managed, the meeting gets shorter rather than longer. And who doesn't LOVE getting time back - remember when I said about making it valuable to the team? There's a concrete example.

Let's walk through each section to identify focus and flavor.

Check-in

This isn't a book about meeting etiquette or good meeting practice, so let me cut to the chase: make your team members feel like the project team meeting is *"coming home"*. Give them a safe, productive, challenging, supportive, and energizing space and interaction.

Engage them as people and grow their commitment to the project.

Because here's the thing, many members of HR are not experiencing this sort of engagement elsewhere in their work-life. Their own bosses are often likely to be *"too busy to care"*, and of questionable managerial skills. If that sounds judgmental, it really isn't, you only have to read the engagement survey results for any HR function, to see what I'm talking about.

And so, it follows that your meeting should start with a welcome, checking how each team member is, getting them centered on the important work you need to cover in the meeting. Make it as humanistic and mindful as possible - after all, your want the whole person to show up!

Plan Review

So, we are gathered and everyone is in the right zone to get going on content.

Here is where you present and discuss the key findings from your daily plan review. By its very nature, this section of the meeting looks at what's happened so far, not what will happen after the meeting - which we'll cover in a moment.

Firstly, the team will review tasks completed since the last meeting. As this is a project team standing meeting, not a full project review, be careful not to go back further unless there is specific reason.

Celebrate completed tasks, particularly if they were a big ask - even a hearty *"well done"* or *"thank you"* here can do wonders. Remember, particularly early in the project, team members will be doing project work alongside highly-pressured day jobs, so you have to put energy into their performance - and live-time recognition is always appropriate.

As always, be careful of a double-edged sword here, particularly if the task was completed in a way that is not what you would have done. There's nothing worse for project team morale than *"well done, but why didn't you…"*

Next, you'll turn attention to those tasks currently planned to be in progress. Are they underway? How are they going? What's getting in the way?

Issues and Decisions

Now that we've turned attention to what's happening, you will:

- Review open Issues
- Make appropriate escalation decisions
- Review Decisions made to resolve Issues
- Capture emerging Issues and Risks and assign for resolution

Your main aim is to keep things tight and not get pulled down into the rabbit-hole of conjecture and *"what if..."*

As you become more experienced with this approach to Issues, Risks and Decisions, the section of the meeting will become smoother and quicker - facilitating quick, in-the-moment project calls on whether to escalate, etc.

Capture it in the Issues & Risks Log, and move on!

Looking Forward

Now that the meeting has covered the meat of what's been happening and where things stand right now, we finish up the project review by taking a look forward.

Once again, the intent here is not to cover everything that will ever happen, but instead to highlight tasks due to begin or complete before the next week - and to check confidence-level for successful delivery.

Secondarily, in this section, we should also look further ahead to see *if, and how, the plan needs to change because of what we've discussed in this meeting*.

Finally, we'll want to look ahead to see if there are any medium-term milestones or stakeholder events that we need to have on radar for project team members.

Reflexive Learning

And with that, we've completed our project team standing meeting. But we're not done yet!

I was introduced to the concept and practice of reflexive learning by Professor Michael West - see *"Effective Teamwork: Practical Lessons from Organizational Research (Psychology of Work and Organizations)"*.

Though it is a simple approach, it is extraordinarily powerful both in the moment and, more so, over time.

Here's how it works.

No matter what, you always stop every meeting or project team interaction 5 minutes before it is due to finish. You then use this 5 minutes to review how the team worked together over the course of the meeting and in the week since the previous meeting. The aim is to identify what helped, what hindered, and what we could have done differently that would have helped. Then we commit to try those things in the coming week, knowing full well that we will review at the next meeting.

The first few times you do this, it'll feel labored and a little awkward - that's fine, learning always is - but, with commitment and repetition, something wonderful happens over time…

The team becomes much better able to anticipate roadblocks and sticking points, and address them in real time. When it locks in, team members can finish each others' sentences!

The first time I saw this happen was on a global process redesign project that I was managing from the UK, with team members in multiple US sites. I'd received feedback from a local SME that, after she'd spent a lot of time and effort providing feedback, she didn't see her input reflected in the working copy of the process. We were about 3 months into the year-long project, and I'd been using Reflexive Learning techniques with the team since Day 1, Meeting 1.

Because of time differences, our project calls were in the evening in the UK, and I was alone in our open plan offices, on the phone and WebEx to the team. We got to the end of the call, and it was time for the learning, by that time a natural part of our working practices.

I shared the feedback with the team and, no sooner was it out of my mouth but a 5-way trouble-shooting conversation erupted between the team members... And, within no more than 30 seconds, they'd isolated how and where the feedback had been folded in, why it didn't seem apparent, who would reach out to the SME to explain (and how), and how they would adjust the core process so that it didn't happen again.

All in about 30 seconds. I literally sat with my chin on my chest it was so fast, efficient and effective. This was what a team could, and should, be!

Live, in the moment, I reflected and thanked them for what they'd just done, and a couple of the team remarked that all that awkward learning stuff hadn't been so off the mark after all! As I headed out to my car after the call, I was grinning ear-to-ear - what a feeling :)

Ever since then, I've included Reflexive Learning in nearly every managerial situation, project or otherwise. This stuff just works, so go do it!

3-Strike Approach

So far in this section, we've covered the importance of involving the team, and structuring interactions and meetings to gain and maintain momentum. At every opportunity, successful Project Managers engage with their teams to move the whole effort forward.

While I'd love to be able to tell you that this works all the time, sadly it doesn't. For whatever reason - self-sabotage, capability, will, internal politics - you will undoubtedly run across the project team member who under-delivers, or doesn't even deliver at all.

In my experience, this is a project management challenge that leans much more heavily on the *management* side of the equation than the project side.

So, if the project team member in question reports directly to you in the formal organization hierarchy, it's time to be their manager rather than their Project Manager, and manage performance.

More likely, however, is that the underperforming team member is assigned to the project while reporting elsewhere. This makes performance discussions more thorny, and it demands that you apply a structured, fair approach.

Note that, in regular performance management, there is always the specter of disciplinary action, and even termination. That represents a whole other level of consequences than simply being kicked off a project, so you have less leverage than a formal manager.

While you may seek to do right by the person, your primary aim is to deliver the project not to turn around the person's overall performance.

It's my choice to practice a 3-strike approach on project team member performance.

First Strike

You notice the project team member missing meetings, not delivering tasks, or delivering tasks incompletely. You may mention it in passing, and course-correct, but at this stage, assume best intent and honest mistake.

Second Strike

We have the beginning of a pattern, though it's too early to know whether it will continue or not. At this stage, mention clearly to the team member what you have noticed, and why it is unacceptable. Listen to any explanation, and offer suggestions or insights into what could be done differently the next time. Set the expectation that the behavior will not be repeated. You may choose to give your Project Sponsor a heads up at this stage.

Third Strike

Now that the pattern has repeated, we must act to protect the project by addressing the underperformance. On a project, we don't have the luxury of waiting to see if it fixes itself. Firstly, inform the team member that the repeated behavior is unacceptable, given the discussion you already had at *Second Strike*, and that you have no choice but to escalate. Secondly, discuss the situation with your Project Sponsor and agree a plan of action involving the two of you, the team member, and the team member's Manager. Your Sponsor is the *"big gun"* here, and you may choose to speak with the Manager in the first instance, depending on your organization cultural norms.

Why the 3-Strike approach is so important

The bottom line here is that any individual assigned to the project team should already have had the expectation set that they would contribute to the team and deliverables, as we discussed in *"Clearing the runway"*. If they're not doing that, they should not be on the team. Period.

The 3-Strike approach handles this situation appropriately and in a timely fashion. If your Sponsor and the team member's manager ultimately decide that the team member should stay on the project - a decision I would hope you were involved in - then make it clear to all involved that the 3-Strike clock has reset, and not gone away!

Involve your Sponsor

Earlier in the book, we described the role of a Project Sponsor, so we won't cover that ground again.

Similarly, we won't revisit the kick-off meeting, aside from noting that there may be a need for a more symbolic kick-off meeting at the start of implementation, that includes a wider sweep of attendees, including Subject Matter Experts, Key Stakeholders, etc. The need for such a meeting, and its structure and content, should definitely be driven by your change management plan, and the norms present in your organization culture.

So, having covered kick-off, let's look at the main ways your Sponsor will be involved during delivery of the project. First we'll get very clear on their most important contribution: *acting as the first point of escalation.*

First point of escalation

We spent a lot of time earlier in this chapter talking about Issues, Risks & Decisions.

Remember, we identified a Yellow-status Issue/Risk as one where the Project Sponsor is monitoring/managing. In essence that means something's come up which the Project Team has tried to handle, but that they can't do on their own.

So they've pulled the Project Sponsor in.

Said differently, the Issue/Risk has been escalated to the first point of escalation beyond the project team.

Now, a highly active, engaged Sponsor will know what to do with that Issue/Risk - and they'll likely work very closely with the Project Manager to ensure resolution.

But humor me for a moment as I suggest that we may, perchance, come upon a Project Sponsor who, I don't know, doesn't really stay up to speed with the project or what's happening. Let's say that this Sponsor is a little, erm, distracted.

This is where one area of project management comes into play that we haven't specifically called out yet: the need to *MANAGE-UP*.

Once again, I'm going to encourage you to standardize and schedule your approach to engaging your Sponsor - you really don't want to operate on a *"drive-by"* approach here.

Depending upon your Sponsor's preferences, you might schedule weekly touch-base meetings to brief on progress - I like to do so immediately ahead of my regular project team meetings, so that I am confident in speaking on behalf of my Sponsor when I cover Issues, Risks & Decisions. This approach also allows for a follow-up *"matters arising"* if necessary, but doesn't assume that you always have to report out the meeting discussion - which can be a significant time and resource saving in the long-run.

Anything more often than this should only really be necessary if your Sponsor is a complete detail-centric micro-manager, and/or the project is operating on highly sensitive content, timelines or deliverables.

For the longer term, I always choose to involve my Sponsor in the review and approval of my regular Status Reports, as discussed earlier in this chapter. By doing so, I provide them with some level of ownership of outward-facing content as well as making sure they are aware of the specifics of progress and roadblocks. Remember, to the rest of the world, they are accountable for this project, so you're really reporting their progress as much as that of the project itself.

There is one other reason for formally involving them in approval of our Status Report: throughout the project, there will be times where they ARE the face of the project, and they must be prepared to do that fully, with full confidence.

It is essential that we give them the support to feel that confidence and deliver on our behalf.

Figure-head, Champion, Compatriot

Away from role descriptions and tactical involvement, we must look at how we rely on our Sponsors. Any Project Manager who wants to achieve success must consider themselves joined at the hip with their Sponsor.

A little while ago, I jokingly talked about a disengaged Sponsor, and I have come across several in my career. Luckily, I've been able to get through to all but a couple, how important their engagement and involvement is.

For the couple where that proved difficult, I relied very much on treating them as I would any external stakeholder. We're going to talk about that in the next section, and even more so in the next chapter, because it's so important.

But for now, as a Project Manager, think of these three reasons you might involve your Sponsor in the project:

- Figure-head
- Champion
- Compatriot

Figure-head

Think of how we asked the Sponsor to present the *"business case for action"* at the Kick-off Meeting. Could the Project Manager have presented that content? Could we have circulated it in a Powerpoint deck of elevator speeches and *"From-To"* diagrams?

Of course.

But there's something powerful in having the leader of an effort speak up at the beginning, middle and end of an effort, particularly for those involved in the work. It's important that we feel we're part of something that is connected to the wider business; that we are appreciated, supported and authorized to take action and make decisions.

In this case our Sponsor serves as a Figure-head for the project, not just at the Kick-off but in whatever way is necessary to let the project team know that they have justification for being active.

Champion

Given that I've discussed at length how our HR function's primary response to projects is a form of self-sabotage, it should be no surprise to know that there will come a point - WILL not *"may"* - where the project comes under fire.

Now, that may be caused by the project being ineffective or inefficient, and if that's the case, it's up to the Project Manager and team to wear the accountability and deal with the fall-out.

But that's not the scenario I'm pointing out here, which is very much more the case of when that self-sabotage is occurring, but that the Project Manager or team cannot solve the issue.

This may occur, for example, when the lead of an HR Center-of-Expertise refuses to play ball with the project team by withholding information or resources. Or when a client-facing generalist HR leader mobilizes to poison their clients against project deliverables and, thereby, creating resistance on the short-, medium- and long-term horizons.

And, yes, such situations do happen. If we don't admit that, we don't deal with it. And if we don't deal with it, we don't get to complain about it, OK?

In such situations, we may need to call upon our Sponsor to intervene, either directly via their authority, or indirectly via their influence.

Of course, this would rear its head via Issue and Risk monitoring, but make no mistake, in these instances, you're asking your Sponsor to get out there, represent the cause, and clear the road so that the project can move forward.

Compatriot

We've looked at how the Sponsor provides figure-head leadership within the project, and representative leadership beyond the project. There's one final area of involvement that sits as a backdrop to the Sponsor's activity: *maintaining troop morale*.

If the norm of HR is to NOT get projects done, then a successful HR Project Manager is, by definition, ABNORMAL.

And, depending on the context and potential impact of the project, that can lead to the Project Manager feeling isolated and alone.

In this situation, the Sponsor is the one person who the Project Manager should be able to reliably call upon to vent frustrations, celebrate small wins, and ease concerns.

How best to involve your Sponsor

So, we've looked at what you'll be asking of your Sponsor while the project is running. How you do that will depend on both your own and your Sponsor's working preferences, as well as operational culture within your organization.

Once again, there is a matter of balance here - how do you keep your Sponsor informed and involved without forcing them to act as a member of the core team? Conversely, how do you healthily distance the Sponsor who wants to dive into tactical activity and detail, threatening to derail the project?

The answer, of course, is to negotiate a working compromise and review its effectiveness on a regular basis.

My own preference is for a regular meeting, on or around any formal status reporting. This is then supplemented by ad-hoc meetings when key milestones and/or meetings are imminent, or if Issue & Risk monitoring is bringing something to the fore.

Whatever your preferred approach, your focus is always to build a strong partnership with your Sponsor as a matter of criticality to project success.

Focus on stakeholders

So far, our list of habits of successful Project Managers has largely focused inwardly towards the project, and at the interface of the project with the world at large, through Sponsor and team.

It's almost time to turn our attention completely outward, a subject so important that we're going to devote the whole of chapter 5 to it.

For now, though, while we're focusing on the Project Manager, I want to draw attention to a mindset that is especially important in HR project management: *keeping the stakeholder in mind.*

To explain this, let me tell you how it *doesn't* work in non-HR projects.

Let's take a house construction project, for example. In this case, the Project Manager is responsible for co-ordinating the work of various contractors and sub-contractors to deliver what has previously been drawn upon an Architect's plans.

At each stage, there may be decisions to be made to resolve issues - and the Project Manager will link up the Architect, Contractor, Interior Designer, Public Authorities and whoever else needs to be involved to make a decision.

While the Project Manager is aware that the building is a house, and that there is an expectation that the keys will be handed over to the occupants at some future date, that's pretty much where the project ends.

At few, if any, points in the project does the construction manager have to consider whether what's being built should change based upon the future needs of the occupants, and even if they do, it's not their job to reimagine the space. That's an issue for the Architect, interior designer and occupants.

In other words, for the vast majority of situations, the construction Project Manager isn't expected to incorporate stakeholder feedback into their own actions and decisions in order to change the very thing they're working on.

But, as we've already agreed: *HR projects are different.*

And to be successful, Project Managers in HR must always keep the stakeholder in mind - which is no small task, given the number of stakeholders we have.

First things first, this means holding outward facing deliverables to the standard of whether they'll do what we need them to do.

For example, if we're training Managers on a new performance incentive, then that training better do that job, right?

Well, yes... And, er, no...

Let me explain.

The project plan tells us to draft, review and approve training materials for managers.

OK. That seems easy.

So, our Learning SME scrums down with our Compensation SME to produce the materials. As Project Manager, we check in with them in our weekly team meeting, and hear that everything's going to schedule.

Cool.

Deadline arrives and, with great pride, the training materials are delivered. Many backs are patted and...

Wait... what we just received turns out to be a 3 hour seminar on the Policy minutiae of the new incentive, including Union negotiation points, and external landscape review.

In an appendix near the end, there's a screen-capture of the online nomination template.

In other words, though the Manager training deliverable has been completed, it is totally *unfit-for-purpose*.

In fact, it's *fit-for-purpose* for practically any stakeholder grouping BUT its target audience.

This is what I mean when I talk about keeping the stakeholder in mind. As a Project Manager in HR, you must make sure that every deliverable, and especially those that face outwards, are fully aligned with their own planned intent.

In our example, there's no way that the Learning and Compensation SMEs should have been free to get to completion without a review of proposed approach, an outline check, 1st draft review, etc.

A preferable deliverable, in this instance, was little more than self-driven online learning coupled to a local cascade of briefings from executive leader on down. Simple.

The bottom line here is that, because we focus so much on intangibles and nebulous outcomes, it's easy for HR projects to become inwardly-focused and forget why we're doing what we're doing, and who we're doing it for. This is why our Project Charter must have clear business vision and mandate coupled, hopefully, to measurable performance indicators.

Our function has been accused of navel-gazing for decades and, as HR Project Managers, we must ensure that we don't sustain that reputation in the one area of work where we have the most control.

Or, in other words, *keep your stakeholders in mind!*

Practice grounded optimism

And so, we come to the end of this chapter. For those keeping score, we've covered 5 habits of successful HR Project Managers:

1. Own the plan
2. Manage the work
3. Manage the team
4. Involve your sponsor
5. Focus on stakeholders

The content of this chapter is going to be home for most of the period your project is in the wild.

"Hang on a second!" I hear you cry. *"What's all this about grounded optimism? That's not even on the list!"*

Well, let's consider this a bonus habit - and while we might call it *"Habit 6"*, I actually prefer *"Habit 0"*, because it comes before everything!

Grounded optimism means starting from *"Yes"*.

Grounded optimism means believing that the project can, and will, succeed.

Grounded optimism means taking action and making decisions in order to move things forward.

Grounded optimism means meeting Issues & Risks with a calm, methodical mind.

Grounded optimism means riding the waves of stakeholder concern rather than being submerged.

Grounded optimism draws upon the facts to assess progress, rather than taking emotional opinion as statements of reality.

Grounded optimism recognizes knee jerk resistance for what it is.

Grounded optimism enables us to get HR out of its own way.

Grounded optimism is *"Habit 0"*.

Have I said enough?

Maybe. But you know HR. And you know the energy that surrounds HR projects. How dreary it can be when the project is failing, and how amazing when success is in reach.

And how painful when our function snatches defeat from the jaws of victory.

If you know successful HR Project Managers, you know that there is a difference to how they do their job.

And I'll tell you now that grounded optimism is their super-power!

9: COMPLETE THE PROJECT

Congratulations, your project has achieved everything it set out to do; take a moment to breathe, and accept that you made it to the end!

So, time to move on to the next thing, right?

Well, not quite.

You see, how we end projects is almost as important as how we begin them, though, naturally, the focus is slightly different.

How we end projects does a few things for the project itself, which is good. But in terms of how we learn for the next project, and every project after that, it's critical to do it well.

Without further ado, let's put this thing to bed.

Measure it

Let me ask you something: *was your project a success?*

And I want you to think before you answer.

Did you deliver the plan?

Did you flex the plan to take account of external events?

Did you produce deliverables?

Did you keep all stakeholders in the loop appropriately?

Did you manage the team elegantly for high performance?

Is your Sponsor happy with how the project went?

To answer my question, you may be considering these, or any other number of areas.

And you would be wrong. Or at least, mostly wrong.

Let's go back to our Project Charter, way back in *"Stage 1: Initiate The Project"*.

The very first section of the Charter is the *"Business Case"*, and we looked at 4 core dimensions against which it should be measured. As a reminder:

- Bottom line impact? (WHY are we doing this?)
- Context for deliverables/milestones (WHAT will be happening?)

- Stakeholder frame-of-reference (WHO will be affected, and HOW?)
- Source for *"Elevator Speech"*? (HOW will we describe the business case?)

More importantly, I encouraged you to identify specific *Business Value Measures* that aligned with these dimensions. And I also made very clear that, for each measure, it is essential to gather a baseline at the outset of the project.

Assuming you identified these measures as indicators, your next step is to measure them right now.

Before you do so, though, let me prepare you for what's about to happen. For many HR projects, the measurement you take when you finish your work will be at, or around, the baseline value. Please expect this, and don't lose heart when it turns out to be the case.

You see, given the intangible nature of our deliverables, nearly all HR projects experience lag-time - the gap between taking action and being able to observe results - in making change happen.

It's easiest to explain this with a couple of short examples.

If your project delivers a new online recruitment portal, then you can successfully claim delivery, but you won't know if it speeds the process, or improves quality of hire until enough people have applied and been hired using the portal. Depending on hiring rates, this could take anywhere up to a year or beyond.

Or let's say your project revamped the career ladders in your company, with an aim of increasing gender and race diversity in your senior leadership ranks. It may take years of hiring, promotions and career development before those representation ratios shift significantly.

This is why it's so important to look at which metrics you are going to be able to measure a) accurately; and b) in a timely fashion.

Lag-time also leads to one other consideration. If the project ends, who will monitor performance over time, and how will it be communicated. In our examples above, who's watching the recruitment and diversity numbers respectively?

We're going to wrap up this chapter by talking about how to make that happen.

Capture it

Have you ever experienced the *"Zombie Project"*? It's the one that you completely finish, and leave behind for done.

Hurrah! Pats on the back, all around!

You move on, explore new vistas, try a new hairdo.

Only, out of the blue, a long time since you forgot that the project folder even exists on your hard drive, someone drops you an email: *"I know you were involved in, can I just ask you to…"*

And, just like that, the Zombie Project is back from the dead, and you're having to devote time, resource, and brain-space to something that ended a long time ago.

A similar situation happens with process-centered projects - there's a very good chance that if you manage a benefits project, you'll end up becoming *"that benefits guy/gal"*. Projects stick in HR, simple as that. Which is why we want to close them well!

How do we make sure that our projects don't become the walking dead? Well, the first thing we need to do is build a really good coffin…

Which, in project management terms comes in the shape of two key tools: a *Maintenance Plan*, and an *After Action Review*. This applies to ALL projects, though it is critical in any software system or process-based project.

Maintenance Plan

Let me tell you a little story…

Back in the mid-2000s, my colleagues in IT realized they were doing a ton of support work for custom-built system solutions, many of which had become redundant but for a small number of *"hold-out"* users, and duplicated functionality in other more-widely used systems. This was doubly worrying because, though IT help-desk activities, content and resource had been centralized, none of the original build projects had thought to prepare content or training for help-desk operatives - and the project teams had long-since disbanded.

As a result, over 70% of their support budget was being spent on upkeep and user-support of these legacy systems.

Said differently, they were living a Zombie Projects nightmare.

From that point on, all projects - including those in HR that had significant interface with IT - had a criteria that a formal Maintenance Plan be signed off by the Project Sponsor before the project could be declared *"Closed"*. Over time, it worked.

Am I saying you should go so far? Maybe, though it always depends on how many projects you run, their complexity, and the scope of impact. Even if it's not a formal plan, it should at least be a line item on the project plan to agree what happens after the project has closed.

And, as you might expect, the breadth and depth of content in your Maintenance Plan will also depend upon your project, so I won't provide a specific template here.

Note that a project has two sets of subject matter. The first is the subject matter of doing the project itself - i.e. the plan, Issues , Risks & Decisions log, Status Reports, Decision Captures, etc. - and the second is the subject matter upon which the Project creates its new product or service - i.e. the processes, systems, products, resources, etc. that the project produces. For the Maintenance Plan, we're not really concerned with the former - it's ALL about the latter!

Here are the specific questions I look to answer with my Maintenance Plans:

1. Who is accountable for the subject matter of the project once the project closes?

2. To whom should any query about subject matter be addressed, if not the person identified in 1)?

3. Who is accountable for learning and development provision for subject matter deliverables (e.g. for New Colleague Orientation design project, who will train People Managers on an ongoing basis post-launch)?

4. Who is accountable for just-in-time support for subject matter deliverables?

5. Who is on-point for any functional intersection (e.g. Finance, Facilities, IT, etc.)?

6. Where will project reference documents be stored? Under what access control limits? And controlled by who?

Your Maintenance Plan should be endorsed as necessary to ensure that it becomes *"the way things are from here on out"* for the project.

And with that done, we've captured the WHAT of the project going forward.

But, for me, the more important factor to capture is the HOW of the project. And this comes in the form of a structured After Action Review.

After Action Review

The term *"After Action Review"* has its roots in military practice and nomenclature.

For our purposes, the After Action Review answers a different set of questions:

1. What did the project achieve?
2. What did the project do?
3. How did it do it?

In many ways, I consider the After Action Review a book-end to the Project Charter, and I tend to have both documents up on screen when working on the After Action Review. On the next page, I offer a simple template for an After Action Review.

A couple of side-notes on this template. First, let's just be clear that we will be talking about Stakeholder Feedback a LOT in the next chapter, so consider that last section a placeholder for what we'll discuss then.

The second side-note has to do with how you summarize your project. Even the thorniest projects fade into memory, so even if you never learn a single thing, it's important to capture things just for the record and posterity's sake!

AFTER ACTION REVIEW TEMPLATE

Summary

- How successful was the project overall? If you only had 15 seconds to describe the impact and experience of the project, what would you say?
- To what extent will the output of the project meet the business case?
- If at all possible, note any Business Value Measures that show appreciable positive (or negative!) impact from project deliverables

Deliverables

- Were all deliverables produced on time and within expected quality and cost boundaries?
- Where did the project miss a deadline or fail to deliver?

Issues and Decisions

- How well were decisions made relating to issues?
- Were there issues that arose that were unforeseen and/or unresolved?

Working Together

- How well did the project team work together?
- What would you do differently next time? (Summarize using STOP, START CONTINUE)
- How available were sponsor/key stakeholders

Stakeholder Feedback

- Consider a short survey and/or interview of key stakeholders
- For larger initiatives, an "impact of deliverables" survey may be appropriate, along with a number of focus-groups
- Use this section to highlight any findings

How do we do this?

Well, remember how we said that the Project Charter, and particularly its description of the Business Case, should provide content for your Elevator Speech of project intent? In a similar way, the After Action Review provides content for your Elevator Speech of project performance and impact.

For example, our project to overhaul recruitment within an umbrella philosophy, can be summarized in the following Elevator Speech:

WE SUCCESSFULLY REALIGNED RECRUITMENT PROCESSES, SYSTEMS AND PRACTICES TO DELIVER *"CANDIDATE AS PRIORITY"*. AS A RESULT, WE DOUBLED APPLICATION RATE, QUADRUPLED OFFER RATE PER APPLICATION, AND RECEIVED 91% ACCEPTANCE FROM 1ST CHOICE CANDIDATES, WHILE REDUCING ADVERTISING SPEND BY 15%

To this day, if anyone asks what that project achieved, that's exactly what I tell them.

There's more, of course, particularly in the information of HOW we did the work, but that's part of our collective learning and not confined to that specific recruitment project.

Celebrate it

We've now ensured that the project's output has the highest chance of success and longevity after the project goes away, by putting in place an appropriately detailed Maintenance Plan.

And we've structured our review of what the project achieved, what it did, and how it did it, using an After Action Review.

By now, if my own experience is anything to go by, you'll be just plain *tired* of this project and ready to move on. This is natural - if you're wired for project management, then the end of things represents a chance that you may be stuck with nothing to do, so of course you want it *over-and-done-with* so that the next thing can happen.

Well, hold your horses, my friend, unless your project failed miserably, it's time to give the team, and yourself, a little kudos.

Celebrating the team

Remember earlier, we talked about the four stages of team development:

FORMING - STORMING - NORMING - PERFORMING

Well, what you may not know is that there's a fifth stage that doesn't get as much attention: MOURNING; although it's actually called *"Adjourning"* in Tuckman's original model.

We know from our first definition of a project that we have been part of a temporary endeavor. Despite this, if your experience is anything like mine, during the project you've built solid, and lasting working relationships - very likely friendships - that will stand the test of time.

So, it's important that we acknowledge the MOURNING phase, reflect on the good, bad, and plain ugly of our shared experience, and practice gratitude for all that people brought to the table.

We know that delivering projects in HR is already a challenge, so if you achieved success despite the odds, you deserve some feel-good energy. And as Project Manager, you also have the responsibility to make sure your team feels the same.

If you're co-located, or can be for a period of time, I suggest some form of relaxed interaction - a team dinner, lunch or even just get together over coffee and cake. These events don't need formal speeches or agendas; it's really all about being together one last time before we go our separate way; even if we simply go back to our offices right next door to each other. This sense of closure is the icing on the cake of a well-delivered project; in many ways, the final deliverable.

At this stage, it's really important that you engage your Project Sponsor to celebrate the team's performance - preferably in person or, at minimum via a written thank you to each project team member.

That said, be careful of one-off, CC-everyone thank you emails from your Sponsor - they can completely deflate the project team at the end of a hard road - not good for the next time they're asked to participate!

Celebrating yourself

Now, I'll keep this brief, because you're probably a little uncomfortable right now and, seeing as how I can't read the room, I might suggest the wrong thing!

So let me state it simply.

If you've been assigned to manage a project in HR and you've successfully got it over the goal line, you've done something many, many others have *FAILED TO ACHIEVE*!

Listen carefully…

WELL DONE, AND CONGRATULATIONS!

There are three important conversations you need to have in relation to the project, each of which has two aims: 1) to successfully capture your specific individual contribution to delivering the project; and 2) to ensure your ongoing growth and development as a Project Manager and HR professional.

The first conversation is your formal debrief with your Project Sponsor. This is not part of your Sponsor's wider interaction with the team, but instead a very focused 1:1 discussion, reflecting on your performance on the project, and your performance in successfully engaging your Sponsor.

There's also a chance that your Sponsor may choose to take your feedback in this conversation as part of their own development - not always the case, but we can but hope that more leaders head in that direction.

The second conversation is between you and your own Manager. Remember, way back in *"Clearing The Runway"*, we talked about how to position the project vis-a-vis your day job, and how you may need to hold your own Manager at distance. Well, this conversation is the follow-up to that. And it's important that your contributions to the project, and your development as a result of the project, are appropriately reflected in your own performance management process, compensation and development plan.

The third conversation is between your Project Sponsor and your own Manager. Depending on your organization culture, it may even be a three-way discussion involving you. The reason for this conversation is simply so that you don't end up alone advocating on your own behalf in performance reviews, career and compensation discussions. Put simply, the organization asked you to manage the project under the leadership of your Project Sponsor. As your performance review is delivered primarily in relation to your job, its worryingly easy for your performance on projects to be downplayed by your Manager.

As Project Manager, it's important to ensure these conversations happen for yourself and for every project team member - quite often, you will be asked to provide feedback on individual team member contribution. Be objective, be supportive, and always developmental. Even if things didn't go right sometimes, make sure the learning continues.

Declare it closed

And so, we reach the end of the road. The project is done.

Do me a favor, will you? Make sure you tell people!

You see, hard to believe as it is, not everyone is deeply aware of the work your project has been doing, the ins-and-outs of Issues, Decisions and Risks, the long nights of cramming to meet deadlines… All of it. Many are blissfully unaware that the project has been running. It may have crossed their inbox one day, they don't remember.

So tell them, with honor, clarity and brevity, tell them!

At minimum, I like to use a Sponsor announcement to the HR function and appropriate external stakeholders to say *"we're done!"* Much as we, as Project Manager, might feel that we should be the voice of this statement, the fact is that we've served at the pleasure of our Sponsor and, as we know, accountability for project outcomes was on their shoulders, even if accountability for project deliverables was ours.

So, they get the pleasure of sharing the message with the world.

To help them do this, take the appropriate content from the After Action Review and, if it makes sense, Maintenance Plan, and use it to craft some core, key messages. Then put that communication content into the media used for such announcements in your organization.

Bottom line your aim is to breathe a well-earned sigh of relief and satisfaction that you're done, just as soon as you see the announcement go out!

10: MANAGING STAKEHOLDERS

We've covered a lot of ground with respect to Project Management: why it's different and difficult for HR, how to increase the odds of success, and specifics on how to actually do it.

In this chapter we're going to look at the world around and outside the project, and specifically, how a Project Manager must focus on managing stakeholders.

Before we dive in though, I want to make something clear: the aim of this chapter is not to teach you how to do Stakeholder Management - that is a subject all on its own, and deserves its own book.

In fact, I would go further and say that, in my experience, capability in project management is not equivalent to capability in change management. I have seen Project Managers who just don't understand the emotional component of change, nor how to flex planning to account for reaction/response. And, I've seen masterful change managers who wouldn't know how to organize tasks if their life depended upon it.

Sometimes, we get both capability sets in one person, which is wonderful - though something of a unicorn in HR - but we shouldn't assume a pre-requisite in either direction.

The inevitable question is how much change and stakeholder management is enough change and stakeholder management.

In this chapter we'll be covering some key insights into managing stakeholders - though I do encourage you to view these these as only the visible tip of an iceberg.

If you plan to manage your change and communication plans as well as the project, you absolutely *must* dive deep into change management frameworks, tools and techniques.

What is a Stakeholder?

First off, let's agree a definition:

A STAKEHOLDER IS A PERSON, GROUP, PROCESS, OR SYSTEM, THAT A) HAS AN IMPACT UPON A CHANGE; AND/OR B) IS POSITIVELY OR NEGATIVELY AFFECTED BY A CHANGE

Ultimately, stakeholder management is ALL about change, and for our purposes, *"Change"* is used to denote any project activity, decision or deliverable.

For many HR projects, it's easy to get lost in the big picture of stakeholder groups.

We can, after all, have an effect on the whole organization.

In fact, allowing ourselves to be overwhelmed by the broad sweep of potential stakeholders is one of our favorite routes into the self-sabotage morass we've discussed throughout the book: *"But what about <insert name/group>, how will this affect them specifically?"*

Let's not play that game, OK? Instead, let's agree to stay *specific within scope*, because it's the only way we don't end up stuck in the mud.

When we parse the definition, we can begin to see that there are types of stakeholder who each have different positions vis-a-vis our project.

A holistic view of Stakeholders

We can think of Stakeholders as forming a major chunk of the context in which our project operates.

When we do so, we can map their involvement in terms of INPUT, INVOLVEMENT and IMPACT.

Take a look at the graphic on the next page - you'll see that, in terms of the project we've already covered INVOLVEMENT stakeholders.

In the graphic, they're represented by the darkest grey box.

A HOLISTIC VIEW OF STAKEHOLDERS

Provides INPUT
to change

CHANGE

IMPACTED
by change

hrprojmgmt.com

Specifically:

- Our Project Sponsor provides strategic DIRECTION

- Our Project Team makes the CHANGE happen

- Our Project Team MONITORS the change

Alongside these core Stakeholders, any HR project must keep track of, and engage with, any or all of the following stakeholder types:

- Change targets

- Executive leaders

- Inform groups

- HR colleagues

- Partners

- Processes

- Systems & data

Of course, the extent to which these stakeholders are involved will depend directly on the subject matter of the project and nature of deliverables.

So, with that in mind, let's turn our attention to the left and right chevrons - those stakeholders providing INPUT to, and/or being IMPACTed by, the change.

INPUT Stakeholders

In fact, we can go even tighter, because your INPUT stakeholders should be addressed as part of your project plan, by stipulating who needs to be involved (and how) in specific activities and decisions.

For example, let's make up a little project to gather and formalize existing processes into a single Standard Operating Procedure database. Take a look at the example plan on the next page.

What do we notice here?

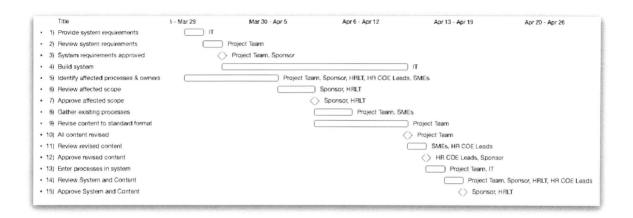

Well, firstly we've indicated where our project team and Sponsor are active - the equivalent of our dark grey box in our *"holistic view"* diagram.

Beyond that, we can see that this project involves a number of stakeholders:

- IT
- HRLT
- HR COE Leads
- SMEs

And these stakeholders are involved in several ways, either providing input such as system requirements and process content, reviewing project deliverables, and, in specific instances, making stage-gate approval decisions.

If your project plan is structured properly, there is little need for a separate stakeholder management plan for INPUT stakeholders.

That said, I do need to point out that you may have change management activities that need to occur alongside project actions.

An example might be having target users trial, and provide feedback on, a pilot system. If so, include those activities on your project plan!

My own preference is to run a change management and communication section of the plan, so that I can keep a close eye on why, how, and when the project is reaching beyond its own boundaries.

Hopefully, this simple example shows how to handle INPUT stakeholders?

And, with that done, we'll turn our attention to those stakeholders who are IMPACTed by our project deliverables.

IMPACT Stakeholders

Even a quick look at our earlier list shows two broad categories of project stakeholders: *human,* and *non-human.*

Even though we're not diving deep into change and stakeholder management here, it should already be clear that stakeholders who live and breathe are where we'll need to spend the most time and focus.

So, let's deal with the non-human ones first!

Non-Human Stakeholders: Processes, Systems & Data

This actually becomes quite simple if you view the world through a process design lens. Bottom line, whatever you're working on in your project will have inputs from, and outputs to, ancillary processes, systems and data stores.

As a Project Manager, you have to keep an eye on each task in your project that requires any such functional interface.

For example, if your project plan calls for learning materials to be in place and available at a specific milestone date, not only do you have to produce the learning content itself, but you have to ensure the technology is available and fit-for-purpose to deliver that content to end-users.

Will your project build that technology? Unlikely.

So it's your assumption should be that the learning management system functional requirements are met by your content and content structures.

You'd be amazed how often these things get missed until it's almost too late - in fact, many implementation fire-fights take place over such missed interdependencies.

As I've already mentioned, we're not diving deep into change management here, and neither are we detailing process design frameworks.

Drawing from both disciplines, however, my main tip for Project Managers here is to work backwards from anything that you want your target population to do as a result of your project - the spreadsheet is your friend here, use it copiously and frequently!

For each action, ask the question: *"How will they do that?"*

Once you have an answer for each action, ask yourself: *"Is the project on the hook for making that happen?"*

If the answer is *"Yes"*, then go make it happen; if it's *"No"* then congratulations, you've identified a functional interface.

I reality, of course, it's much more likely to be somewhere between *"Yes"* and *"No"*, in which case the question becomes *"What's our part of making that happen?"*

In so doing, you've taken an IMPACT and worked out what INPUT you need to make it happen.

As a result, and as we've seen earlier, you can now treat that as an activity/ milestone on your plan - working back from when it needs to be in place, who will deliver it, and how long it will take them.

Before we move on from this subject, let me just say that you can go crazy trying to manage the work on the far side of a functional interface, so I strongly advise you not to try. Position your project as a customer to your partner, making your needs and expectations clear, and then use Issue & Risk monitoring to assess confidence in delivery. If the functional interdependency is very great, consider adding a representative to the project team - for example, on a number of projects I have run, HR and IT have been joined at the hip.

Now that we've covered non-human Stakeholders, it's time to turn towards the lifeblood of HR: *People, groups and organizations!*

Human Stakeholders: People, Groups & Organizations

Way back at the start of this book, we talked about how HR projects are different, about how we deal with intangibles, and how we often self-sabotage project deliverables.

The root cause of all these aspects of project management in HR is that we deal with the most chaotic, unpredictable resource in the organization: *PEOPLE.*

Worse than that: *People who we are forcing to change!*

But rest easy, as we're not diving deep into change management and communications, we're not going to get too lost in transition curves, the n-stages of grief, nor complex theories of human motivation.

It's not People, it's Stakeholders.

Why is that?

Stakeholders form a network of relationships around a change - i.e. they are *within scope*.

They may be end-users or targets of project deliverables.

They may be informal and formal leaders in the organization

They may control organizational resources (staff, budget, infrastructure, etc.) necessary to design, implement and maintain project deliverables.

And, in terms of our project, we are simply concerned with the best approach for making stakeholder relationships serve project deliverables.

Let's continue working through our list from earlier in this chapter.

Change targets

These are the people and/or groups who will be required to change their actions and decisions due to project deliverables.

For HR projects, we can think of them as end-users of systems, or participants in processes.

Depending on the project, they may be a specific sub-division of your company (e.g. region, business unit, department, etc.), or they may be a type of role (e.g. Individual Contributors, First-line Managers, Leader of Leaders, etc.), or an employment class (overtime exempt, hourly paid, temporary, bonus eligible, etc.), and the list goes on and on.

Now this may seem obvious to you, I mean *"targets are targets"*, am I right?

Well, sort of...

You see, the reason we need to identify the groups affected, and how they are each impacted, is because there is overlap between groups.

For example, let's say that Jane is a Senior Director in Finance - at any given time, she will be an employee for sure, but she may also be a First-line Manager, a

Leader of Leaders, part of a Regional organization, in the Corporate Center, in a global role, etc.

Now, let's say we have a project dealing with adjustments to the pension plan... Jane is definitely impacted by the project deliverable as an employee, but she's ALSO impacted wearing any number of hats due to her group identification. She may also be an INPUT Stakeholder if Finance is involved in the pension redesign

And, if we don't take a holistic view of our stakeholders... Well, all of a sudden, Jane gets hit by a scatter-gun barrage of communications, some of which apply to her, while others completely miss the target.

Bottom line: we have to detail who our targets are, and how our project deliverables affect them in terms of role and responsibilities, before we can hope to craft an integrated change management and communication plan.

Key tools: *Stakeholder Map, Stakeholder Readiness Assessment, Change Plan, Communication Plan (inc. training)*

Inform groups

Beyond our change targets, there are any number of other groups that need to be briefed or made aware of your project deliverables. Because they're not your priority, you run the risk of falling into a *"leave-them-be"* mindset. And this might be totally appropriate. However, if your project covers any subject area that could be considered remotely sensitive, it's always worth considering the extent to which you might need to deploy *"Here's what's happening... though it doesn't affect you..."* communications.

For example, run an exploratory project on restructuring the overall compensation approach, and I can almost guarantee the rumor-mill will spin up expectation of across-the-board pay cuts!

Key tools: Stakeholder Map, Communication Plan

HR colleagues

An inform group all on their own, your HR colleagues have to be treated as a separate entity, with their own communication and involvement needs. Consider the impacts of project activity and deliverables upon each function within HR, and upon individuals within those functions.

For example, your relocation expert will need very different communication about an onboarding design project than will your employee relations lead.

As we discussed earlier in this book, be careful that you don't end up using project involvement as your main strategy to address your HR colleagues, as we know where that ends up... My preference is a clear, well-articulated communication plan that is shared and updated regularly, so that my HR colleagues know what to expect and when to expect it.

Then... Deliver that plan!

One particular factor to keep an eye on here is the briefing and awareness of project deliverables to your front-line HR Business Partners. We still work in a prevailing context that *"HR sucks, but my HR rep is OK"* - so you have to know that HR Business Partners will be the voice of your project deliverables, whether you like it or not. Make sure they are on the same page of the same hymn book!

Key tools: Communication Plan

Partners

If your project involves anyone outside the HR function, without inviting them onto the core team, you have to consider those partners as individual stakeholders.

In a project to define core headcount budgeting, for example, we might have a partner within Finance who provides historic dollar data.

We might, for example, engage a 3rd-party training company to deliver workshops on one of our project deliverables.

For partners in the input chevron, it's important to set clear expectations and manage delivery of input. For the impact end of the equation, look to specific, planned, timely communication.

Key tools: *Project Plan, Communication Plan*

Executive leaders

There's no doubt about it, an executive leader in any target group - or even a target adjacent group - can derail your best implementation plan with as little as a rolled-eye in a briefing meeting.

Like it or not, the organization confers upon executives both formal status and authority. And the people of the organization largely comply with that formality AND ascribe informal status and authority to executives.

For HR projects, we'll typically consider all executive leaders to be stakeholders, though some are more important than others, as we're about to find out.

Key Stakeholders

While we can keep an eye on all stakeholder groups, there are some to whom we need to pay greater attention.

Often, these are executive leaders, though not always - we might consider the example of a workplace union rep who we need to advocate on behalf of project deliverables.

Regardless of formal or informal position, these people have a *"make or break"* influence over the successful implementation of project deliverables in a significant section of the organization.

There are two main ways they can do this:

1. Damage or block implementation
2. Influence people in the organization to change, or NOT to change

Knowing this, we have to admit the reality - we MUST manage Key Stakeholders actively as INDIVIDUALS and not just as a member of a group.

For example, if we are preparing a generic Senior Leader briefing presentation for onward dissemination, that likely isn't enough for a Key Stakeholder - who we should brief directly instead with customized briefing materials that better reflect the Key Stakeholder's needs.

By now, you should already be feeling that managing Key Stakeholders can be a lot of work. And you'd be right.

Firstly, it is resource intensive, due to the individual focus, and need for proactive management.

Beyond the resource demand though, is the *"political jeopardy"* inherent in even identifying someone as a Key Stakeholder.

Sure, we might accept that all stakeholders are not created equal, but *"make or break"* is hard to define in purely quantitative terms, and it isn't necessarily a function of position or resource power. Once we begin to consider influence we're into the territory of fuzzy logic.

As a result the biggest risk here is that ALL stakeholders are designated as key - and your implementation will, at minimum, slow down - though there is significant chance that it could grind to a complete halt if you try to keep everyone briefed about everything. And, if that kind of sounds a little like our HR self-sabotaging behaviors, it's no coincidence…

The final challenge in managing Key Stakeholders is that you have to ensure a structured, methodical approach to interactions. This takes a similar discipline to the management of Issues & Risks, with tracking of activity and stakeholder state, and contingency plans if it looks like they are not supportive.

That all sounds well and good - and is meat and drink for a seasoned Project Manager - however, the rub comes because the majority of activities with Key Stakeholders are informal and one-to-one, so any attempt to track or manage formally can be perceived as bureaucratic and a waste of time.

The trick, of course, is to manage all stakeholders with the *appropriate* level of focus.

HOW MUCH FOCUS?

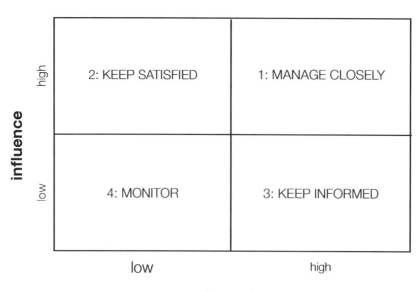

1. **High influence, high impact**
   Fully engage as reinforcing sponsors, involve in decision-making process

2. **High influence, low impact**
   Keep satisfied with appropriate high-level communication, requires less detail

3. **Low influence, high impact**
   Keep informed, consult to help with details, brainstorming and piloting

4. **Low influence, low impact**
   Invest minimal effort, provide broad, high-level communications

hrprojmgmt.com

An appropriate level of focus

Rather than ask whether a stakeholder is key or not, it's easier to assess them against two dimensions: *INFLUENCE upon the project*, and *IMPACT of the project*.

When we take our list of stakeholders and do this, we end up with a 2x2 grid as seen on the previous page.

From this, we can see that there are 4 broad groupings of Stakeholders, running in priority order 1-4 as indicated.

For most projects, I consider group 1 to be my Key Stakeholders - where I'm going to spend a lot of time and focus.

Sometimes, depending on the project itself, I might stretch to include group 2.

Groups 3 and 4, however, rarely need individual attention, and can be folded into your regular communication planning.

Assessing Stakeholder State

In introducing this chapter, I made clear that we would not be diving deep into the world of Change & Stakeholder Management and Communication Planning.

But I do want to pull something out of those particular toolkits, because it will help you frame and guide your project activities and deliverables: *Stakeholder State*.

Put simply, we have to assess how our Stakeholders feel about the project and deliverables right now, and also how we need them to feel at some future date, such as implementation.

We use 3 levels to describe this:

- **SUPPORT:** Stakeholder states their support and actively advocates on behalf of the initiative/project/program
- **NEUTRAL:** Stakeholder states a "wait and see" position or no position is known
- **OPPOSE:** Stakeholder states material reservations about the initiative/project/program

Note that, in some models, Support is broken into Support and Advocate - however I choose to simplify here, and bake advocacy into the action plan requests of Support-ive stakeholders. Once again, the aim is not to assess state, but use that state to advance the project!

Any stakeholder with influence over the project and/or change targets has to be at minimum *"NEUTRAL"* about project deliverables, though we'd obviously prefer them to be at *"SUPPORT"*!

In general, our aim is to move OPPOSE-ing stakeholders to at least Neutral. If we come across a recalcitrant stakeholders who are unlikely to ever change their opinion, we may simply have to resort to an assessment of the maximum risk they represent for project deliverables.

If the worst case scenario looks or sounds like *"bumpy road, but we'll still get there..."* then we may have to swallow the pill that someone doesn't like what we're doing.

Tracking Stakeholders

In closing this chapter on stakeholders, I'd like to share one more thing from my toolkit: *Stakeholder Tracking.*

Much like Issues, Risks & Decision tracking, I use a spreadsheet-based tool to list and track my project stakeholders.

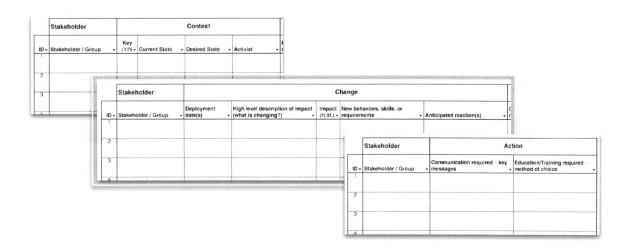

As you can see, there are three section to this tracker: *Context, Change & Action.*

By going long-form, it's possible to spot crunch points, and who's on point for each stakeholder.

I call this role an Activist, because they'll be active on the project's behalf with a particular stakeholder/group, and we need them to care enough to make things happen. That said, I know in some circles, the term *Activist* carries negative connotations, so if there's an alternative terminology that works for you, go for it! Some alternatives that I've encountered include: *Advocate, Agent, Champion, Enthusiast, Promoter, Spokes-person, Messenger,* etc. though I have to say that none of these really speaks to me in the same way as *Activist.*

Note that involving members of HR as Activists on behalf of the project is a great way to involve without adding them to the project team.

Whoever you choose to deploy as Activists, and whatever you call them, ensure that they know that they are accountable for *"delivering"* the stakeholder in the right state at the right time.

Can you, a member of the project team, or your Sponsor be an Activist? Sure, though be careful that you don't duplicate or usurp someone else's activity

.

11: BEYOND THE PROJECT

As we draw things to a close, I'm conscious that project management is something of a *"gateway drug"* for other areas of structured working.

We're going to talk about some of those in this chapter, but I want to repeat my caution from the *"Before you do anything"* chapter: *Project management is designed to deliver projects, so be careful of deploying it wholesale to non-project based work.*

It's much better to pull specific aspects into other work where they make sense. For example, I frequently use Decision Capture notes in my regular work with clients, so that we stay on track and accountable for performance.

In other arenas, I've found the Stakeholder tracking approach and toolset useful as I mapped out specific marketing campaigns.

All in all, do what works, but don't follow the protocol so slavishly that you end up chasing your own tail.

As I say, the job is not to produce the perfect project plan, it's to deliver value!

So, with that said, let's look at some of the areas that will inevitably arise just as soon as you start doing project management in a committed way.

Program & Portfolio Management

I touched on Program Management in the *"Project Management Basics"* chapter, defining a Program as a collection of Projects within a single strategic aim.

An analogy I like to use:

PROJECT = PLANE

PROGRAM = AIRPORT (MULTIPLE PLANES)

PORTFOLIO = AIR TRAFFIC CONTROL (MULTIPLE AIRPORTS)

Specific techniques vary at each level, however fundamentally it's all about tracking progress and surfacing/addressing Issues, Risks & Decisions at the appropriate level.

Alongside this, however, there's an extra level of Status Reporting, as a Program/Portfolio Management Office won't be maintaining plans, so they'll take status reports from each project and then aggregate to a single view of progress. Red/Yellow/Green status is pretty much the norm.

That said, it did take me a year of reporting out this way from a PMO before a key stakeholder told me they were Red-Green color blind! From that point on, I didn't just report using colored circles, but put a R/Y/G inside the circle as well. Which worked just fine, until one of our overseas locations told us that R/Y/G didn't work with them as a language frame, so we started using thumbs up - thumbs horizontal - thumbs down on a colored circle, which seemed to work for all involved!

One of the key benefits of Program and Portfolio Management is integration of project deliverables by timeline, budget and impact group.

For example, when we took a Portfolio-wide view across an HR Service Delivery Initiative, we spotted that each project had slated First-line Manager training for the same week; over 12 hours when aggregated. Each training session had at least an hour dedicated to the background of the overall initiative and business case, 4 hours in total. Yes, that's right, a third of the training was repetition of our *"Why?"* and not our targets' *"What?"* and *"How?"*

We were able to head off that train wreck long before it happened by staging the training over a longer period, and collapsing similar content into an introductory briefing.

Change & Stakeholder Management

I'm really, really conscious that I kept holding this subject at bay in the last chapter. And I want to be very clear that this omission wasn't because I don't value the subject, but instead the contrary: *beyond core project management skills, it's the most important foundation for success.*

For that very reason, I faced the choice of all-or-nothing in writing this book and, to stay focused, decided to hit the high points only.

By it's very definition, every project delivers change. And every project has stakeholders.

You can use project management techniques to manage change and stakeholder management. But change and stakeholder management is NOT project management.

So, your action is to learn how to do it *alongside* project management, or find a partner who already knows how to do it! If you're not well-versed in change management approaches and toolsets, consider adding a capable change and communication resource to your project core team.

If you don't address this area on your team you may find it being spun-up outside the team by nervous key stakeholders - and, believe me, the last thing you want is a parallel change management project!

HR Transformation

And with that, we come full circle to how HR changes. At the start of the book, I consciously took the time and space to indicate the underlying beliefs, behaviors and attitudes that cause so many HR projects to fail.

It's important that we look in that mirror often and with complete candor.

So, let's say we did that, accepted that we needed to do things differently, and fully adopted a project management mindset.

Maybe not all-of-a-sudden, but pretty soon, we would be seen to be making good things happen well.

In other words HR would have transformed a central aspect of our offering, and challenging widely-held stereotypes of our function, both internal and external.

Do that enough, and we would begin to enjoy it; high performance becomes addictive.

As a result, alongside specific project performance, we would also find more members of our HR function adopting structured working practices, moving past the *"I'm busy"* to *"I'm adding value"* - another critical aspect of transformation.

Increasingly, what seemed impossible to achieve, would be proven to be achievable, and our function's capacity, capability, and impact would increase... alongside a corresponding increase in expectations and accountability.

You want that, right?

So, it stands to reason, if you want to ride the wave, commit to the first step: *growing your project management mindset!*

12: SUMMARY OF KEY TOOLS

Project Health Check

The Project Health Check is a simple, 5 question assessment of root cause issues affecting project delivery. Can be deployed on an individual project basis, or as an aggregate across multiple projects to identify systemic themes. Can be deployed at any stage of project life-cycle, and/or on an ongoing basis.

Project Charter

As discussed earlier in the book, your Project Charter serves as your vision, intent and roadmap. Due to its nature, and the extent to which it is used to engage and influence key stakeholders, my preference is to use a word processing-based Charter, which may then be distilled into more presentation-based software.

Know for sure that your Project Charter will be printed out by most, if not all, of your stakeholders, and must be ready to stand on its own without you being there to explain and defend it. Therefore, your software of choice must allow necessary formatting to impress/reassure key stakeholders.

Project Plan

At the simplest level, a project plan can be thought of as a *"to do"* list. On steroids. It provides the detail that underpins core questions: *"What's going to happen? When? Who's going to be involved? Who will it affect?"*

Specifically, the project plan consists of activities, decisions and milestones. It may also include information on assigned resources and impacted stakeholders.

As a practical tool, the project plan can be produced on paper, in a word processing document, a spreadsheet, a slide presentation - although each of those software solutions require some compromise in planning functionality, and introduce inefficiency in updating the plan on an ongoing basis.

The tool of choice here, is specific Project Planning Software.

Project Planning Software

As we've just discussed, various families of software can be repurposed to produce and maintain project plans, however doing so always presents some level of compromise. For this reason, I strongly suggest installing, and learning to use, a specific project management software tool.

A quick search on Google will show there are a multitude of solutions available, from the venerable, industry-standard Microsoft Project® through to cloud-based apps. As you assess the right solution for your needs, consider your use case - it's easy to be wooed by complex functionality and flashy bells and whistles - which are actually designed for super-users in highly complex initiatives. Remember that, when it comes to project management, most HR functions are at the most basic of capability levels and, as a result, most higher level functionality won't be used.

One particular area of focus when it comes to this is in the use of online dashboards and report-outs. Much like HRIS analytics suites, dashboards promise much by way of effectiveness and efficiency but, sadly, often fail to gain traction amongst HR stakeholders at anything deeper than *"at-a-glance"*. For this reason, be careful of any project management solution that requires executive stakeholders to drill-down/click-through to status information.

In fact, my best advice is always to be asking yourself: *"Can this be printed out?"* - because, somewhere, an executive HR Admin is being asked to do just that with your immaculately prepared soft copy!

By way of information, this book was written and published using Mac OS X, and all project diagrams, plans and charts were produced in OmniPlan, which is my tool of choice in managing my client projects.

Gantt Chart

A Gantt Chart is the core representation of the project plan, flowing from left to right as a timeline. Often referred to as a *"waterfall diagram"*, a Gantt view starts in the top left and flows right and down until the final milestone in the bottom right corner. Along with each discrete activity, decision and milestone, the Gantt chart also depicts task dependencies and overlaps.

A note of caution: Gantt charts, while second-nature to an experienced Project Manager, can be confusing to stakeholders beyond the project team.

Project Calendar

This is a distillation of key activities and milestones from the project plan into a more readily-digestible calendar view. Using this view enables easier communication, and alignment with typical HR stakeholder preferences to be diarized at all times. A Calendar view of the project plan can be produced within most Project PlanningSoftware, however the translation is not always formatted cleanly, and often requires significant rework in (e.g.) Powerpoint.

Issue, Risk & Decision Tracking

This tool is an ongoing working document used by the project team to monitor active issues and risks, and record resulting decisions (though detail of decisions is captured in the supplemental Decision Capture tool).

My preference is to use a single spreadsheet to track Issues, Risks & Decisions, simply because I've never found the need to go to a more complex, automated database toolset. Any software must allow for easily formatted print/export options and, once again, online dashboard functionality can prove rate-limiting when it comes to sharing with executive stakeholders, particularly those within the HR function.

Decision Capture

The Decision Capture tool provides one of the key knowledge management functions for any project. It is a statement of record, that can be used, reviewed and revisited as necessary. As the Decision Capture will often include long-form text, it is better served by a word processing toolset than spreadsheet or other database format.

Stakeholder Tracking

A Stakeholder Tracking tool maps all affected stakeholders (both individuals and groups), their current and desired orientation to project deliverables, assigned project activists, and any key messages that should be reinforced. Much like Issue, Risk & Decision tracking, this tool is used as a living document, and at any stage should present the current landscape in reference to project delivery.

Once again, my preference for Stakeholder Tracking is to make use of a spreadsheet. Any software tool must allow for easily formatted print/export options and, once again, online dashboard functionality can prove rate-limiting when it comes to sharing with executive stakeholders, particularly those within the HR function.

Change Management & Communication Plan

The Change Management & Communication Plan is either a standalone project plan, or a subset of the master project plan, so typically makes use of a similar toolset. By definition, change management and communication is more likely to touch stakeholders on a regular basis, so prior flags about use of calendar presentation of plan are doubly applicable here.

Status Report

A Status Report is a readout of project status and forecast. When I am in total control of project report out, my preference is a word processing-based report, with presentation-based a distant second. With that said, this is the one document that is most likely to have its format dictated from external to the project - for example, by a Project Management Office - in which case, be careful of doing double duty, ending up maintaining two formats. If there is an expectation for the project to report out in one style, then make that the style for ALL reporting of status.

After Action Review

As discussed earlier, an After Action Review is both a process and a document. My preference is to capture the summary in a word processing format, with read-out via presentation software only if necessary due to accepted practice.

Document Repository

As we draw this summary of tools to a close, I wanted to make quick note of Document Repositories specifically, and document control in general.

There are two over-arching reasons to make use of a structured approach to the storage and maintenance of documents. Firstly, there is the ongoing work of the project, where multiple people may be editing single documents, and/or need to access the latest version at all times. Secondly, at any point, internal project documents may need to be used, or provide content, for stakeholder-facing communications. Bottom line, there is always a need for a single, authoritative source of information.

It is easy for any project, and particularly Project Manager, to fall into the trap of storing project documents locally, with all the inefficiencies and disconnection that results.

For this reason, I strongly advise using a shared Document Repository for both working and legacy project documents. A quick search of the web will reveal a multitude of potential solutions. As mentioned previously, be careful not to shop for higher level functionality at the expense of basic blocking and tackling.

The key functionality that you'll need alongside basic file storage is that of User Access Control (i.e. - who can see, edit, create, and/or delete documents) and Version/Edit History Control (i.e. who made what changes to what document? Can we roll back to a prior version?)

This latter functionality is very important in terms of managing live project documents and also by providing a route to forensic assessment during the after action review.

Alongside automated version history, however, I strongly recommend adopting good document control within individual documents, using version numbers, author, change control, etc. Once again, while we're in the heat of battle, it's good to know at a glance where we've been and why!

13: WHAT HAPPENS NEXT?

So, we are reaching the end of this stage of our journey together, and what a ride it has been!

I do hope that you've learned something that you can apply right away and, even if not, I'll be satisfied if I have provided even one opportunity for you to check in with your own project management mindset.

As I said way up front of the book, I believe that the potential of *people*, *teams* and *organizations* is ours to unlock, and that the better able we are to get things done, the sooner we will be able to act as a force for positive change in the world.

Project Management, particularly when delivered in HR, is not a theoretical endeavor - even if we sometimes run the risk of turning it into one, by way of an avoidance tactic! In every sense, getting things done in HR is a contact sport; relying on interactions, influence and insight.

There is simply no way to deliver projects in isolation.

For this reason, I'd like to invite you to join my IMPROVING HR MASTERY COMMUNITY at improvinghr.info, so that we may continue our journey together as you, and I, accumulate more and more real world experience of making things happen in HR.

Together, we are building a community of HR professionals who know how to get things done, and get them done well.

At the site, you'll gain FREE access to tools and templates that I've described throughout this book, as well as those from my other books. They're yours and you can use them right away.

Beyond tools, though, when you choose to become a member of the active community, you'll be able to participate in discussions, join regular trouble-shooting calls, and enjoy members-only access to future events, both online and face-to-face.

To register, just visit *improvinghr.info/join-improving-hr-now* and choose the right option for you!

That said, I really would like you to join the community - we have great things to do together!

THANKS

As for any of my books, records, or other creative work, my first and greatest thanks go to my family, who are gracious enough to tolerate me being a little detached, and willing to let me spend enough time *"off-planet"* to bring things together. Jane, Elise and Kyra - thank you, I love you more than you can know.

For this book especially, I am thankful to former and current colleagues and clients; each of you have informed my journey, and blessed me with learning more profound and deeply-felt than I suspect any of you truly know. It is my honor to have worked with you.

Bizarre as it sounds, I am thankful for the forced separation we have all endured due to COVID-19. True, the book began before lock-down, but it most surely was brought to fullness and fruition amidst face-masks and social-distancing. The objectivity of this period cannot be understated, and provided a gift of focused immersion for which we writers would gladly trade body parts.

Finally, I thank each of you in Human Resources. We are often the punchline to too many lazy jokes, and suffer more than our fair share of insults and stereotypes. At my heart, I believe people come to the function because they want to help, and want to make a difference. It can be hard to do the right thing amidst the slings and arrows, but that doesn't mean we shouldn't keep doing it. Thank you for being a commitment for change, and for making people, teams and organizations better!

Vince
Waterford, CT - April, 2020

Vincent Tuckwood is an award-winning consultant and coach with a track record of delivering high-value, high-impact projects and programs in Human Resources. Known for seamlessly blending vision & strategy with on-the-ground implementation, his writing draws valuable insights and anecdotes from nearly 30 years of success.

After 2 decades with Pfizer Inc. on both sides of the Atlantic, Vince stepped out on his own in 2010, founding his own independent consultancy, View Beyond LLC:

Email: vince@viewbeyondllc.com
Web: viewbeyondllc.com